The Me
Everyone's Guide
And Car

Dedicated to Elmer and The Fat Man.

Acknowledgment

No mechanic can truly exist without a coterie of loyal customers. I wish to acknowledge all my customers over the years for their faithful use of my services. For spatial reasons, I can't list every single one of them here, although they all have played a part in my success. But I do wish to personally acknowledge some of my most loyal and supportive customers. Some have moved on to far-away lands, and a few have passed away, but I remember all of you.

Many thanks to:

Dean Ornish	Kathy Wetmore	Dave Goldstein
Amy Freeman	Jill Pickett	Bob Carberry
Ann Makris	Paul Huber	Amée Atkinson
John Bradley	Toby Tate	Bob Baier
Patricia Faber	Pat Murphy	Rose Glaze
Barry Moore	The Szabos	Fernando "Buz" Cabrall
Rita Ettlinger	Jim Decker	Diane Stonecipher
Emma Kowalski	Gene Forsythe	Tanya Reischman
Sharon Davis	Mike Monro	John Carter Brooks
Ray Zukaitis	Jude Wiggins	Bob Snyder
Nancy Randall	Jimmy Olson	Ann Stafford
Don Sanders	Mary Myerson	The Millers
Gail Means	The Catretts	William Mordica
Craig A. Remkus	Linda Luttrell	Linda Toyota
Lee Kennedy	Randy Roach	Liz Mengel
David Morris	Susan Kolbe	Don Spinelli
Dan Smith	Micki Fine	Richard McDugald

INTRODUCTION

With the cost of buying a new car rising almost astronomically, purchasing a used car and maintaining it makes more sense than ever. As soon as a new car is driven off the lot, thousands of dollars are immediately lost. Many thousands more are lost through depreciation during the first three years of ownership. When factoring in additional costs (such as higher insurance rates and higher interest payments on new cars), the notion of purchasing a used car becomes even more attractive. And the benefits of car maintenance is obvious: an ounce of prevention is worth a pound of cure (and is infinitely cheaper).

But when given such information, I have often been told by my customers, "Look, I know nothing about cars! I just drive them and put gas in the tank. What business do I have buying a used car and maintaining it?" My response is that even though you may know very little about the mechanical inner-workings of an automobile, you know much more than you might think. You have been driving cars for hundreds (or thousands) of hours and innately know quite a bit about them. You know about strange noises that the car shouldn't be making. You know something is wrong when the steering wheel is shaking. And you know countless other things that are right and wrong with a car. Maybe you can't technically describe these things, but you do understand when a car is running correctly and when something is wrong. You can put all this inner knowledge to use when attempting to purchase and maintain a used car.

Of course my customers have an advantage that most people don't have. When they have finally decided on purchasing a particular car, they pay me to personally check it out before they buy. After they purchase it, they have me give them advice on maintaining their car (believe it or not, I actually show them what they can do themselves and what they should leave to me). Unfortunately for you, I run a one-man repair business in Texas. Unless you live rather close to me, or plan on driving rather large distances, this last option is unavailable to you. That is why I have written this guide. Inside is much of the information I have acquired during the past twenty-five years of maintaining cars and checking out used cars for purchase. Some of this information will make you laugh, some will make you want to scream at others, and some may even make you scream at yourself. But all this information will help you pick out a good used car and show you how to maintain it. Remember, EVERY CAR DRIVING DOWN THE ROAD IS A USED CAR.

Table of Contents

Chapter 1

WHERE TO BEGIN-
WHAT CAR TO BUY?

To begin at the beginning, you must first decide what type of car you will be looking for. If you have already decided on a model, you might skip this chapter, although I'd advise you to scan the two lists inside as they might prove useful. But if you're not sure, read on. Deciding on a particular model involves a great deal of personal preferences, but the decision is not a simple one and my advice may help make it easier. First of all, you must decide whether you are going to look for a particular make and model of car, or whether you're going to look through a range of cars before deciding. My advice is to begin with a range of cars. Decide whether you want an economy car, a mid-range car, a luxury car, or a sports car.

Once you have decided on the range of car you wish to purchase, you have to narrow the field down into which particular vehicles are best suited to you and your pocketbook. There are many ways to help make this decision, but each has it's own advantages and pitfalls. This is where buying a used car truly becomes an art. The most obvious way to begin is to ask your friends about experiences they've had with their own vehicles. If you network this out with their friends, the coverage of many different car models will be assured. You can then get a personal perspective on various models by asking the information you feel is relevant-such as how the car rides, it's acceleration, it's repair record, how it's paint job holds up, or any other aspect you're interested in. This approach has the advantage of giving you direct personal information with no middle men involved, but you often need to know the person rather well to get true information. And some people don't wish to seem a fool for buying a lemon, so you may get false praise from using the personal route. But it is a good way to begin.

Then there are the numerous books and magazines extolling the virtues of various car models, all with their own merits and pitfalls. On the face of it the consumer oriented magazines would seem a very good choice. They give information on models such as gas mileage, average repair record, resale value, and so on. But the problem here is the reliability factor-what are their figures based on? Are repair records based on a six month period when the car was new and you have no idea what occurs when it's five years older? And how was this information collected-by phone calls to owners, or independent mechanics' records, or by a survey ultimately funded by the car manufacturer itself? I personally had a customer who was telephoned by a supposedly independent company that was doing a survey on car model satisfaction levels. But when she began to describe all the problems she had with her own model, she was hung up on and her negative information was never recorded.

So you can use the information in these and other periodicals to give you some ideas of which model to pick, but you certainly don't want to treat the information as the whole truth. Which brings me to the next method-ask a good mechanic (or see what type of car he or she drives). If anyone knows automobiles, it's a good mechanic. But then you ask, what really is a good mechanic, and how can I find one? Maybe your search for a good mechanic will end up like Diogenes' lifetime search for an honest man, but the following information should greatly decrease the odds of looking in all the wrong places.

Most people innately know what a good mechanic is-someone who gives them accurate information on what needs to be done to correctly maintain or repair their car. Someone who gives them honest, accurate estimations on the cost of such servicing, and someone who really understands their particular model of car. In picking a mechanic to discuss the merits of various car models it is this last aspect that is most crucial. For when having your car repaired, you may want to use a mechanic who specializes in your particular model, but when deciding which model to purchase it may not be such a good idea. This is where Diogenes' quest for honesty applies-someone who specializes in one type of car has rather large ulterior motives in convincing you to buy that model, as they make their living servicing them. When deciding on which cars to look at, it is much better to talk to an all-purpose mechanic who services a range of cars. You may want to use the specialist when ultimately paying a mechanic to check out the car you wish to purchase, but you're better off talking to a renaissance mechanic if you need help in deciding which types to look at.

So how do you find this illusive all-around mechanic? Unfortunately it's not as simple as looking one up in the local phone book and setting up an appointment. Although we live in the information age, it is not commonly acceptable for mechanics to charge for general advice on cars. I personally spend a great deal of time with my own customers discussing the merits of particular car models for them to purchase, but I do not present them with a bill for services rendered. The charge is more indirect-they are my customers and I service their cars for remuneration. In my own case, this usually makes for very good advice-for if I give them bad advice and they choose a car that turns out to be a lemon, I would in all probability lose them as a customer. And as I have an unlisted telephone number and only acquire new customers through word of mouth, this bad advice would spell certain doom.

This is where your friends can again assist your quest for good transportation-ask around who knows a good general mechanic. Of course you may already know a good mechanic or may even have a relative who is one (assuming you're still on speaking terms, relatives being what they are),but it never hurts to better your information base when purchasing an item as important and expensive as a car. Once you've located this mechanic, explain who referred you to them and how you're looking for both a good mechanic and a good used car to buy.

Have the following information ready (or at least as much as you are sure of) to give to the mechanic when discussing which type of car is for you:

Information To Tell Mechanic When Deciding On Model

1.Approximately how many miles you drive in a year.

2.Whether you drive mainly highway miles or city miles, or a combination of the two.

3.Whether gas mileage is a big factor in your choice.

4. Whether a diesel car is a viable option or you just don't like them.

5.How much money you wish to spend.

6.Whether luxury items like power windows and electric door locks are important or meaningless.

7. Whether body or paint damage means a lot or a little to you, as the price of cosmetically damaged cars are lower even if they run perfectly.

8. Which is more important to you-a newer model car, or an older model with the same or less mileage on it. For the cost of newer model cars even with relatively high mileage will be much higher than an older model car that may have the same or even less mileage on it.

9. Whether you can pay cash for the car or have to finance it, as cash can both facilitate the deal and often help lower the final agreed on price.

10. How long do you plan on driving this car, either in terms or years or mileage.

4

11. Whether you want an automatic transmission or a standard transmission, and how rigid this choice is (in modern times many people do not know how to drive a standard and have no interest in learning).

If you're extremely lucky, your mechanic may even know of a car for sale that generally fits your needs (remember here that we do not live in a perfect world and your perfect notion of a car may not even exist in a brand new model). I was once so lucky that upon waking up one morning, I discovered a beautiful station wagon parked in my driveway with a note and keys. A customer of mine had recently inherited a luxury car and wished to sell the station wagon. It just so happened that my wife was looking for a station wagon of that very same model, so we bought it. But if you're not so lucky (and admittedly that was the first time it had ever happened to me) the next chapter may help lessen your feelings of uneasiness about where to look for the type of car you have chosen.

Before finalizing your decision of which model or models to look at, here is some personal advice on cars you should attempt to avoid:

What To Avoid When Choosing Car Model

1. Unless you are a car collector and plan on looking at your car rather than using it for dependable transportation, avoid car models that are no longer in production. This includes both entire car ranges that are not longer sold (such as the ill-fated Yugos) and models whose manufacturers are still in business but whose particular models are no longer being made. Contrary to what salespeople or owners may tell you about the availability of parts for such cars, it is often very hard to near impossible finding parts for these cars. And there are usually good reasons these models are no longer in production, due to mechanical and engineering problems built into them—problems you should avoid.

2.Avoid high mileage cars unless you are paying a very low price and you don't plan on driving the car very many miles per year. The only real exception to this is if you're looking at certain European diesel cars which regularly run reasonably trouble-free for two to three hundred thousand miles.

3. Avoid cars that have been poorly repainted, with runs, drips, or cracks, unless cosmetics and resale value mean nothing to you. Cheap

paint jobs only worsen over time, and are extremely expensive to repair correctly. The car must have all the old paint stripped off to fix a bad paint job, and then be completely repainted. This is a very expensive procedure.

4. Avoid cars that have been in wrecks (other than fender-benders with only superficial exterior damage) as much hidden mechanical damage may lurk inside them. Even a professional mechanic may not be able to ascertain all this hidden damage. A wreck may slightly bend transmission or suspension parts, so that the car runs well now, but may require very expensive repairs thousands of miles down the road.

5. Spend a little time researching the popularity of the car you've chosen. If you've chosen a model that everyone is just dying to get their hands on, you're going to pay premium price. You may want to rethink or modify your choice. As an example, sports utility four wheel drive vehicles are presently very hot models going for extremely high resale prices. Maybe you'd never even use the four wheel drive. A conventional pick up with a nice cap on the back might suit your needs perfectly for a lot less money.

6. If you have had the good fortune to discuss your car buying decision with a mechanic, take the advice you're given on which models are loaded with pitfalls and avoid them at all cost. I can think of a few personal customers who ignored my warnings about buying a certain model car and purchased it anyway. They thought the deal was just too good to pass up at the time, but they were full of regrets later on. A little inside information can go a long way if you take advantage of it.

Chapter 2

THE QUEST-WHERE TO LOOK?
(*or* WOULD YOU BUY A USED CAR
FROM THIS MAN?)

Once you have decided on which type of car you wish to purchase, you must discover where to find one—It's Out There Somewhere! There are many ways to go about this, but we shall begin here with used car lots, as you may not be completely sure which model best suits you. Used car lots often have many different models of cars, and the trial and error of actually driving them may help you decide which is best for the amount of money you want to spend. And even if you are sure about your model choice, used car lots often have a few of these models in stock to choose from.

You might start screaming,"I've been to used car lots before. I hate their high pressure sales tactics! They're so dishonest!" But you must remember, YOU CONTROL THE SITUATION. You are the one spending money, and you can walk away any time you want, as long as you haven't signed anything. If you can't stand the salesman given you, ask for another (and I am not being chauvinistic here—for the used car sales world is still a very male dominated area with little or no females involved at the sales end). You are directly paying the salesman, as they are all on straight commission. If you remain in control of the situation and they don't assist you in the way you wish to be, you can walk away and they will not make one cent.

This is where a little knowledge about used car lots can go a long way. First, you must realize how you are going to pay for this car. If you have no other option than financing the car through the lot itself, you are at a great financial disadvantage. As an example, I once checked out two used cars on the same day for two different customers, Fred and Sam. Both cars just happened to be the same exact year and model station wagons. Both were being sold by used car lots, but Fred was paying cash, while Sam had neither cash or a good credit rating. Sam was financing it through the lot itself. Even though Fred's car had thirty thousand less miles on it than Sam's car, Fred paid twenty five hundred dollars less than Sam did for his lot financed car. If you have any type of access to borrowed money—be it relatives, friends, banks, or credit unions—attempt to do so when purchasing a used car. Because if you have to finance a car through a lot, it is seen as a big service by them, and one that you will pay dearly for both in terms of interest rate and the price of the car itself. As the saying goes, money doesn't talk, it screams; and in the used car business it almost breaks the sound barrier.

But then you may well ask, how do I choose which used car lots to go to? Now this depends on the status of your search itself. If you are uncertain as to which exact model to choose, go to a large general purpose used car lot that has many different types of cars. Then you can make a better hands-on decision about which car you like, and you may even discover a model that interests you on that lot. Or if you are rather sure about the model you're looking for, you may go to a used car lot that specializes in that model, or is affiliated with a new car dealer that sells that particular type of car. Only here you must be warned that specialization often drives the price of that model up. Sure, it's easier just driving over to the new car dealer of the model you've chosen and inspect their stock of used vehicles that's next door, but ease of discovery and savings of money do not often go hand in hand. Some of the best deals I've seen in used cars purchased by my customers were from dealer used car lots that were selling another manufacturer's model. They were Toyotas purchased from a Ford dealer's used car lot, Hondas bought at a Chevrolet dealer's used car lot, Fords bought at a Toyota dealer's used car lot, and so forth.

Always remember, a little of your own time spent searching at not-so-obvious places may save you quite a bit of money in the end. See the whole search as an adventure, go to a few lots and see if your dream car is hiding there. Some people drive out into the country to lower overhead lots, some stay within city limits and try their bargaining skills there; it's a game pitting your bargaining skills against the salesman's. You might spend an afternoon at three or four lots and see nothing; or you might hit a lot on the first try that has your car and a very hungry salesman who needs even a small profit sale desperately. Remember, used car salesmen make their living strictly on commission, and they know that ninety percent of the "be backers" (people who say they will come back to deal tomorrow) will never return to their lot. Sure, they'll try to get as much money as possible from you at first, but if you show resolve in the bargaining process, they will come down rather than risk losing you (and your money) forever. Their motto for good bargainers is "better a small chicken than an empty pot," and they will deal down if you force them to. Some used car lots even employ people whose sole job is to stop customers from walking off the lot in the hope of making some sale at least.

When at the lots, compare models and asking prices to see what's out there (but always remember that a lot asking price is strictly a highly inflated "sucker" figure which leaves them plenty of downward room to play with). This comparison will give you a good general feel of what shape the used car market is in for your particular model, and give you a base upon which you can begin the bartering process. And I might note here that I treat lots that sell used rental cars the same as other car lots, although you will find that they allow no bartering. They have a fixed price on each model that is non-negotiable. But would you really want to buy a car that may have been driven by hundreds of different people and maintained by minimum wage "mechanics"?

Of course if you have your own ability to pay for a used car (either with cash or through a private financing institution), you may want to try what many people consider the best alternative—buying a used car directly from the person who owns the car. Many people worry about the condition of cars at used lots, figuring that if a car was a good deal and didn't have any real problems with it, the owner would sell it personally. They would not have taken the much lower price one always gets when trading the car in at a lot. People feel (and sometimes they are correct) that cars at lots are problem cars which their owners dumped for a little cash just to be rid of them. This is not always true—I have had knowledgeable customers purchase good used vehicles for reasonable prices at used car lots. But it is an aspect of used car lots that must be taken into consideration. As any wise person might think, if this car is such a good deal, why is a professional sales person needed to sell it? Of course some people have to deal with used car salesmen because they can only get financing through the lot itself. But aside from a very small percentage of people known in the automotive trade as "car queers" (those who get a kick out of hanging around car dealers and get strange pleasure out of the actual deals being cut) not many people relish the notion of spending any of their own personal time dealing with used car salesmen and their various gambits.

So how do you discover the whereabouts of someone personally selling the type of car you're looking for? As previously mentioned, make sure you tell all your friends and associates that you are looking for a good used car, because your chosen car may be right under your nose. People get too old to drive, people die (as morbid as it may seem, I have personally gotten a very good deal on a motorcycle whose owner had passed away from a heart attack), people move out of the country, people decide that one car will suit their lifestyles just fine and they opt to sell their second car, and so on ad infinitum. And such people tell their friends and associates that they are attempting to sell their vehicle long before they start spending money advertising the car's sale in the local newspaper. These are the cars everyone dreams about finding, the cars with no hidden problems, the cars whose owners have decided to sell for whatever reason and give someone a golden opportunity. If your networking pans out and you hear about such a car, make haste and check it out quickly. Such deals rarely stay around long.

But if your luck doesn't hold here, you can start with the obvious- look at the used car section in the local newspapers. And some modern-

10

day newspapers have free (for those on the buying end) computerized services that can save you time. There are also many "swap sheet" and "car trader" magazines which are commonly sold in convenient stores and book shops. Many of these contain vehicle pictures so you don't waste your time driving across town only to discover a rusting hulk or a smashed tomato awaiting you.

Only before making that phone call or drive in search of your dream car, here is a list of what you should avoid at all cost when looking for a place to buy:

What to Avoid When Looking
1. Avoid the "paper" used car lots. These are lots that will finance anyone on planet Earth. They give credit to anyone and usually have signs all over the place advertising this. They can do so because the cars they're selling are all "iron" (as in junk iron) and the lots have paid very little for them. The cars are often bought in mass, with the lot paying perhaps four thousand dollars for ten cars. The lots may not even know what is wrong with these cars themselves, they just take each car's purchase price as a down payment. Then they have no money themselves invested in the car, and see how large a weekly or monthly payment they can wheedle out of the buyer. And if the buyer misses a payment, they will just repossess the car and sell it all over again. There may be a decent car hiding amidst the rubble, but only a discerning mechanic should even attempt to find it.

2. Attempt to avoid individuals who claim to be selling their own personal car but in reality are selling someone else's vehicle. They may say it's their wife's car, or their husband's car, or even the old standard, it's their friend's car who had to move out of the country. One of the oldest tricks in the book is for a private individual to be selling problem cars for a used car lot by using his own personal advertisement in the newspaper. Since most people prefer to buy a car through an individual, this often makes the sale easier and removes any legal warranties that would be in effect if the car was actually sold through the lot. To avoid this, ask whose name is on the title of the car, and if things don't match, don't even consider the deal. And if the deal finally makes it to the money exchanging point, be sure you or your money lender has seen the actual title. If things don't match there, just stop the deal.

3. Never attempt to enter a used car deal (either with lots or private individuals) naked with no idea of what your chosen car model is worth. You wear clothes going to the deal, so make sure your mind is not naked

as well. As previously mentioned, shop around some to see what price ranges exist for your model. As an example, I once met a person who had just purchased a two and a half year old sports car at a very large volume used car lot. He had just paid five hundred dollars more for this car than a new one cost, and at an outrageously high interest rate to boot. There are no laws that limit the price of any used car deal (only laws covering maximum interest rates), so be prepared with knowledge on price.

4. Avoid used car lots and individual sellers who handle "chop shop" cars. If you're on a lot, and you see many cars that have obviously been in wrecks and were cheaply repaired, walk away. These are the chop shop dealers who buy wrecked, flooded, and stolen cars. They fix them up cheaply, sometimes even making one car out of the parts from two or three other cars by welding them all together. These chop shops then try to sell these poorly repaired cars for hundreds or even thousands less than the going rate for undamaged models. The same advice follows for individuals selling these chop shop cars—walk away from them. Even if you can't see obvious physical evidence of damage or cheap bondo repair work, the car may have hidden internal damages or may have been in a big flood and will electrically self-destruct later on. Always ask to see the car's title, because if it says RECONDITIONED on the title, it is a chop shop car. It has been totalled by an insurance company and sold as is. That is all the title RECONDITIONED means. It does not mean the car has gone through some high calibre reconditioning service checked out by the government. It is really a title that says, "Warning, look at some other car instead". The only thing that the government checks is whether any parts used to fix the vehicle by the seller were stolen parts, as the seller of a reconditioned car must furnish valid receipts for repair parts used. There are too many chances to take when buying a car that has been previously totalled by an insurance company, so stay away from reconditioned cars.

Chapter 3

ZEN AND THE ART OF USED CAR BUYING

CHECKING THE CAR OUT YOURSELF

When you discover a car that interests you, it's time to physically check the car out YOURSELF before going any further with the deal. Even if you don't plan on spending much time checking out the car personally and wish to leave most of the dirty work to your mechanic, you still need to spend some time checking it yourself. As an extreme example, I once checked out a car for a couple who were meeting me at the car's location. They were running late and didn't arrive until after I had almost finished checking out the car. Upon seeing the car, they told me to stop wasting time examining the car, because they hated its color and would never buy it. They had never even seen the car before sending it to me for a mechanic's check, wasting time and money needlessly.

But before getting into the actual process of checking out a car, I must delve in a little philosophy. As the saying goes, the only perfectionist who will be happy is the one seeking out mistakes. We do indeed inhabit an imperfect world, but somehow we manage to keep on going and hopefully have a good time at it every now and then. You must apply this same life philosophy when checking out a used car. Sure, there may be dings and scratches on the outside (looking in the mirror I for one am certainly no longer in showroom condition), but the car itself can have many years of faithful service left. You need to discover the following: 1. What problems you discover in a used car are telling you to walk away and look for a different car. 2. What problems mean this will cost X amount of dollars to fix and you will deduct it from the price you will pay for the car. And 3. What problems are just nagging little nuisances which you just live with (like those mysterious little pains in your body that come and go as you age). In the rest of this chapter I will attempt to guide you through these decisions; showing you what means walk away from a car, what means dicker more over the price, and what means it's a very good car. Being a perfectionist mechanic (at least during working hours, though my wife might argue that point), I will be stressing the negatives when checking out a car so you won't be taken advantage of by the seller. But always remember there are positive things you are looking for also. And if all else fails, think about how many hours of work at your job it would take to earn the same amount of money you can save when buying a used car instead of a new one. That's enough to sober up anyone.

I realize that people have various levels of mechanical aptitude— from those who only put gas in their tank to people who change their own oil and perform their own tune-ups and brake jobs. In this section I discuss check-out procedures for this entire range of aptitudes, beginning with the simplest and working up to the more complex. But don't be disheartened if you feel competent only with the basic procedures, because they can give you much information on whether the car is truly a good buy. And for those of you who have a high level of mechanical ability, please don't be a riverboat gambler trying for an inside straight and finalize the deal after you complete every check. You should still send the car to a professional mechanic to be checked. The small amount of money you pay could still save you from huge regrets later. I have even seen mechanics who have paid other mechanics to check out a car which possibly had problems they were not specialized enough to be sure of (doctors are not the only ones living in the age of specialization).

Tools to Bring to Your Check
A. Tools for Everyone.
    1. A notebook and pencil.
    2. A flashlight.
    3. A small screwdriver.
    4. An old rag or paper towels.
    5. An old blanket or towel to lie down on (optional).

B. Extra Tools for the Ambitious Mechanical Person
    1. A small rolling car jack and a pair of jack stands (low usage ones are commonly available at discount auto stores for as little as thirty five dollars if you need a set).

    2. A small tool box collection including screwdrivers, pliers, spark plug socket and ratchet, a magnet, and a tire iron four way to remove the car's tires in case the car's removal equipment is missing.

    3. Any test equipment you may own-such as a voltage/amperage meter, a dwell meter, or a radiator pressure testing pump. But don't rush out and buy new equipment unless you plan on gambling and not using a professional mechanic to do a final inspection.

    4. A small tarp or other suitable material for use when crawling about under the car.

Checking Out The Car For Everyone
    The ABSOLUTE FIRST THING you must do is to ask the person selling the car if you can have a mechanic check out the car before you

decide on buying it. Even if you are a riverboat gambler and aren't going to use a mechanic you must ask this question. Because if the seller will not give you the right to a mechanic's check, there is something bad hiding under the hood. If they will not allow a mechanic of your choice to inspect the car for any reason, as logical as it may sound, DO NOT BUY THE CAR. They may tell you they can't allow it for insurance reasons, or because another person is coming in half an hour with cash, or any of a thousand different reasons. These reasons may be cogent ones when used in the bartering process over the car's price, but they hold no water when checking out the car's mechanical worthiness. If you will not be allowed to have your choice of mechanic check out the car, go no further with this particular car. But don't let the preceding information turn you sour at this early stage of checking out a used car. Because almost everyone will allow you to use your own mechanic. This information merely allows you to weed out the few individuals who will not let you.

If you are dealing with a salesman, be cordial to him as you begin to check out the car, but basically ignore everything he says while you go about your business of checking the car. Salesmen have far too many games to play for you to waste your time attempting to discover what he says is true and what is just a line of nonsense. As an example, he may show you small body damage in a car, hoping you will then trust his honesty and not look under the car to discover a rusted-out floorboard. Or he may tell you that your chosen model is known for weak automatic transmissions and attempt to steer you to a different car (and one that he will make a higher commission on).

If you are dealing with an individual selling their own car, you should act friendlier when checking out the car, but still don't put too much weight on their information. Unless you happen to be dealing with an honest person who will show you everything that they know is wrong with the car (yes, Virginia, there are still honest people around). You don't want to insult an honest person, but you must remain on your guard, and don't waste too much time trying to figure out if the owner is full of baloney or a shining samaritan. And unfortunately there is a lot of baloney out there today.

As people vary greatly in both their mechanical abilities and interest, the following section on checking out a used car yourself is divided into THREE PARTS; A. THE ABSOLUTE MINIMUM APPROACH. B. THE APPROACH FOR EVERYONE ELSE. And C. THE EXTRA APPROACH FOR VERY MECHANICAL PEOPLE.

A. THE ABSOLUTE MINIMUM APPROACH

This approach is to be used by people who wish to spend very little time of their own checking out the car. They prefer to let their chosen mechanic do the brunt of the dirty work. I truly advise people to spend more time and energy than this and heed the saying "If you want something done right, do it yourself." But I also realize there are those of you who either don't have the time or the inclination to expend much energy of your own checking out the car. Some of you may feel uncomfortable checking out a car and would like a mechanic to do most of the checking (although I advise you to read approach B and discover how easy it really is).

First, take my previous advice and politely ignore whatever the seller may be telling you while you go about your task. Take a deep breath, exhale and relax. Start the car up, and see if smoke pours out of the exhaust, meaning major engine problems and time to look for another car. LEAVE THE CAR RUNNING THROUGHOUT THESE CHECKS. Then look at the car in direct sunlight and examine the paint job to see if it's all one color. If the car has been repainted this will often show up in direct sunlight. Look for rust on the car's body on the bottom insides of the doors, around the windows, and around the wheel wells. If you see places where the metal is rusted completely through, think about another car. Rust in cars is often like cancer in people—the beginning of the end.

Open and close all the doors and trunk to check for correct fit. Look inside the trunk for standing water or rust stains, as this is often the result of a rear-end collision. And believe it or not, stand back about fifteen feet from the car and look at it from the front. If you see that the tires on one side stick out of the fenders and the tires on the other side stick further inside the fenders, the car has been in a massive wreck and should be avoided. Then turn off the car and look under it. See if large quantities of liquids have dripped on the ground. Small leaks can be left to the mechanic to uncover, but large leaks mean look elsewhere.

If you feel good about the car after these checks, restart the engine and go for a test ride. Try to drive the car for ten to fifteen minutes in a combination of city and highway driving. While you are driving check the following:

1. Turn on the heater to see if it works. Do the same for the air conditioning, if so equipped.

2. Watch the temperature gauge (if equipped) while driving in stop and go traffic, and see if the car is running too hot.

3. See if the steering wheel shakes or pulls to one side when driving at highway speeds.

4. If the car has an automatic transmission, make sure the gears are shifting smoothly and not jerking. If the car has a standard transmission, make sure the clutch is not slipping by accelerating hard at highway speeds.

5. Listen for unusual clanking or roaring noises coming from the engine when both accelerating and driving at highway speeds.

When you are finished with your road test, stop the car and again look under the car for major leaks (old leaks may have been cleaned off by the seller and your road testing the car at highway speeds will bring them back out into the open). If the car interests you, write down what you have discovered or what you may have questions about. Then give this information to your mechanic and let him do a thorough check as described in Chapter Four.

B. THE APPROACH FOR EVERYONE ELSE

This approach for checking out a used car should be used by everyone besides those using the minimum approach (and if you minimum people are still reading, think about changing your mind and using this approach instead). Even you extremely mechanically minded people should begin with this approach, and merely add on the checks included in section C after you have finished section B entirely. Take a deep breath, exhale slowly, and start looking at your chosen car. Begin by looking at the following major areas where car problems are hidden. Don't waste time checking out many smaller non-critical problems first, only to later discover a major problem that will cross this car off your list.

1. ATTEMPT TO DISCOVER IF CAR HAS BEEN IN A BIG WRECK

Look at the car in direct sunlight if at all possible. See if the car is all one perfectly matching color. This is important for all used cars, but especially important for later model cars. If you are checking a car out that is only one to four years old, look very carefully for any sign of paint mismatching or paint overspray. Look under the hood, inside the trunk, and inside all the wheel wells for paint overspray. Because any signs of painting on a late model car indicates the car has been wrecked. As an example, I had a customer who was looking at a two and a half year old car, which had obviously been repainted fire engine red. The seller told her that he didn't like the original color red and so repainted it a brighter shade. When I personally checked out the car, I discovered some very major body damage to the car that had only been repaired as cheaply as possible. And to add a little humor to the situation, while I was checking it out, a man pulled into my driveway in a car that was the same exact year and model. It was also the same shade red, and it had never been repainted. The seller of the car had not even changed the shade of red used!

Many older model used cars will have been repainted whole or in sections (if involved in fender benders), and such damage repair may lessen the value of the car. But such damage in a late model car should be avoided unless you're buying the car at a very cheap price, and if you have a mechanic who you trust fully to check out the car for further damage. Most people looking for a late model used car are searching for a "cherry", and should avoid those with signs of repainting.

After assessing the paint job, stand back about fifteen feet from the car and see if everything looks straight. Look at the car from the front, the back, and both sides. Check the alignment of the doors, trunk, and hood to make sure all the seams are even—so there isn't a quarter inch gap on one side of the hood and an inch gap on the other side. Now turn the car's wheels so they are pointing perfectly straight. Stick your hands behind each front wheel and get a rough estimate on the clearance between the back of each tire and the car body (do this by measuring the distance from the middle of the tire's back side to the closest part of the car's frame). This distance might be one finger's width or four finger's width, the actual size doesn't matter. What matters is that both front tires have the same amount of clearance. Because if the left front tire has two fingers of clearance between the tire and the wheel well behind it, but the right front tire has four fingers of clearance, THE CAR HAS BEEN IN A LARGE WRECK. Do the same check for the rear wheels to see if the back of the car has been in a wreck large enough to bend the entire frame/suspension system. This entire check will only take you a minute or so, but it can easily discover a hidden lemon— something to avoid at all cost.

Then stand back fifteen feet in front of the car and look at the tires again. See if both front tires are in the same position relative to the car's body. If you discover that one tire is sitting further outside its fender than the other tire, the car has been wrecked sideways and is bent. As an example, Joe once brought me a car to check out. Joe was nuts about the car, but he said it felt a little funny driving at highway speeds. It wasn't shaking or pulling to one side, it just felt "a little funny". When I stood fifteen feet behind the car (the distance is to give you a good perspective) I saw that the entire car body was bent a foot and a half to the right of it's true center. Needless to say Joe didn't buy the car, but he did waste quite a bit of his own time needlessly. So be sure to use your eyes sharply when checking the car's body alignment from both the front and the back. It will take you less time to check than you just spent reading how to do it.

2. CHECKING THE CAR FOR MAJOR RUST PROBLEMS

As previously mentioned, rust in a car is often like cancer in people—the beginning of the end. The time and money spent battling cancer in people is both mind-bogglingly gigantic and proof of mankind's noble side. The time and money you would spend attempting to stop the cancer of rust in a car would also be gigantic, but it would be proof of nothing more than a very bad decision. For as Neil Young croons, "Rust Never Sleeps", it just keeps doing its dastardly duty of eating away metal twenty-four hours a day. Those living in the northern climates know all too well the ravages rust can perform on a car. It can turn an otherwise perfectly running car into a pile of rusting junk that even those who care little about how a car looks would be ashamed to be seen in. But northerners are not the only ones who are affected by rusting cars; everyone can easily fall prey to the devastation rust can bring to a car (excepting those few living in near-desert arid climates where the relative humidity and average rainfall levels are extremely low). As an example, Kristin moved to Texas from a northern state with a four year old car. The car looked superficially fine, but rust was beginning to surface on the car's exterior. Within a year and a half the car was literally rusting to pieces, with one door actually falling off its hinges if opened. Most people think of cars in Texas (with the exception of those cars living near the salt breezes of the ocean) to be relatively immune from rust due to mild winters. But it is humidity that really feeds the fire of rust, and on planet Earth high levels of humidity are everywhere (just feel grateful you're not driving your car in a rainforest). Granted, there are ways to prevent rusting of a car (which I discuss in Chapter 6), but you do not want to purchase a car in which rust has already gotten a strong foothold.

So begin by looking for obvious signs of rust on the car's exterior body. Concentrate around the windows—look carefully at the front and back windshields where rust often shows up first. Then open the doors and look at the bottoms (both inside and out) for any signs of open rust or paint bumps. With these bumps, you must get the permission of the seller to do the following: use your small screwdriver and push firmly on the bumps. If they break open and go through the metal, the car is rusting from the inside out. Once a car has begun to rust from the inside out, it is a car that you want to avoid.

Then open the trunk and look inside carefully with your flashlight for any signs of rust. If you feel industrious, you might want to pull aside some of the paneling inside the trunk and see if rust lurks behind it. Look in the bottom of the trunk under the spare tire for rust or signs of water leakage (you might have missed these signs that the car was wrecked in your earlier check). If you notice large signs of rust or pools of standing water, it's time to look for another car.

The last major area to check is under the car, so get out your old blanket and slide under the back. Shine you flashlight all around the body looking for obvious holes or rusted sections. But don't feel out of the woods if you don't notice anything wrong. Look for evidence of relatively new areas of undercoating (that dark sticky asphalty substance used as a sealer). If you find such areas, scrape a little off with your screwdriver and examine it. If there is a mixture of rust pieces in it, the car is rusting out. One of the oldest tricks in the book is to cover up rust with undercoating, so the car looks ok to the potential buyer. You may think, "Oh, the rust is sealed with undercoating, so it will be fine", but don't be fooled. Once rust has begun in a car, undercoating is useless in the long run. This is why most professional undercoating companies will not give a warranty when they undercoat used cars that have already started rusting. They know rust will continue along its merry way, and in due time the floorboards will turn into road viewing port holes.

3. CHECKING FOR A FLOOD DAMAGED CAR

As most cars today have entered the computer age, flood damage to a car is more serious than it has ever been. Many parts of a car do not mix well with water, such as automatic transmissions which can be ruined with even a relatively small amount of water mixed in with transmission fluid. But electronics are even more sensitive to water, and the damage done can be much more insidious than with purely mechanical parts. As an example, I once went over to my customer Jim's house to repair his car. The car's engine would turn over and over, but just would not start. I noticed the fuel pump wasn't working, so I replaced it. Then the car was getting plenty of gas but still wouldn't run. To make a long story short, I worked on the car for hours before the car started to get the best of me and curses began flying. Jim (who works at home with his computer) came out of the house and asked what was wrong. When I explained all the problems I was having with his car, he curtly replied, "Didn't I tell you the car was flooded out three years ago? The water came in through the top of the rolled-down windows." It had taken fully three years for the water damage to entirely destroy the electronics of his car. Water damage can be death to a car's electronics—it may take days or months or even the relatively rare case of years—but it is definitely something you want to avoid.

So first of all, use your nose. Get inside the car, roll up the windows, and do some serious sniffing. If you smell musty, mildewy odors, start to become wary. Look under the rugs and seats for either damp or moldy sections. And as ridiculous as it may sound, look up!

I once checked out a car that smelled funny to me as soon as I sat inside and rolled up the windows. My customer had not noticed the smell because the car had been aired out before she had looked at the car, and mild perfume had been used by the seller to disguise the mildew odor. I looked up at the roof of the car (the section technically known as the head liner) and noticed many water stains. The head liner itself had been reinstalled poorly, so I bent it a little and looked inside with a flashlight. Mold was everywhere, leaving me with the conclusion that the car had been completely immersed in water. Needless to say, my customer ended up buying another car that I inspected the next day.

If your nose makes you suspicious, and you pull up part of the rug only to find rust everywhere, you need to tap the floorboards very hard. Because if the floorboards are solid even though they're covered with surface rust, the car has been flooded. The rust in itself means little if it's just surface rust, but it is symptomatic of much graver problems that flooding can cause. Many car manufacturers bolt their ECU's (computer control units) to the floorboards underneath the rugs and seats, and if they get wet VERY STRANGE THINGS can happen to the car in the near future. I have seen cars with flood-damaged computers that would only run backwards, or whose headlights would come on when the brakes were engaged, and many other odd occurrences which would have you laughing in stitches if it was happening to someone besides yourself. But don't let this information sour your search for a used car, because in reality very few cars I have ever checked out had been badly flooded, and floodwaters are very common where I live. Just spend a few minutes looking and smelling to ensure that the car you have chosen hasn't been for a swim.

4. CHECKING FOR MAJOR MECHANICAL PROBLEMS

The next step in attempting to weed out a bad car is to actually start the car and search for major mechanical problems. And there is a very good reason for not actually starting the car until now. The oldest trick in the book when selling a mechanically problemed car is to warm up the car's engine before the potential buyer (you) shows up to look at the car. It is always best to check out a used car that is ice cold-when you open the hood and touch the radiator top it should be completely cold or at least luke warm at best. Many major mechanical problems can show up when you attempt to start a car that is ice cold. You may have to crank the engine for minutes if the car has major engine problems and is ice cold (such as bad valves, bad pistons, or a worn-out camshaft). The same warmed-up car may start with relative ease, thereby masking very serious problems. You should always attempt to examine a used car ice cold, but I realize that this is not always possible. The person selling the car may have driven the car to you for a look, the car may be on a used car lot that makes a practice of warming up all the cars on the lot first thing every morning, or someone else may have just finished taking a road test in the car. BUT YOU CAN AVOID HAVING TO CHECK OUT A COMPLETELY WARMED UP CAR by taking my previous advice. First check out whether the car has been in a major wreck, whether the car has major rust problems, and whether the car has been flooded out, as I have described in sections one, two, and three. This serves the dual purpose of checking out things you need to do anyway, and allows the car to cool down.

Turn the ignition key and see how easily the engine comes to life. If the car is fuel injected, it should start right up without pumping the accelerator pedal. The starting circuits in fuel injected cars are all computer driven and should require no assistance from the driver other than simply turning the key. Most cars today are fuel injected and should be extremely simple to start, unless they have a problem. But if your chosen model has a carburetor instead, it is not often that simple. Those of you who have owned carburetored automobiles certainly have fond memories of the little idiosyncrasies that they could have when starting cold. Even an otherwise perfectly normal carburetored car may require two and a half accelerator pumps to start; it may need the engine cranked for a couple seconds and then have the accelerator pedal pumped twice to get the engine roaring; or it may need some other strange ritual of seemingly magical combinations to get it going first thing in the morning. (Even though much grumbling has come from both the general public and mechanics themselves about emission controls and fuel injection complexity in cars, it has at least made starting cars a much simpler, more reliable process.) So if an unwarmed-up carburetored car will not start right away, you might seek advice from the seller on what exact "trick" needs to be done to get the engine going. You shouldn't worry about what combination of cranking and pumping this involves, unless the "trick" is to open up the car's hood and spray starting fluid in the carburetor.

When the engine roars to life (though not too loud a roar if the exhaust system is in good shape), glance out the back window. See if large amounts of smoke are coming out of the exhaust system. Blue smoke is indicative of burning oil and metal; black smoke is indicative of unburned gasoline from too rich a fuel mixture; and white smoke is indicative of steam from the engine burning off its own coolant. Many perfectly good cars will give off a very small puff of any colored smoke when started after an overnight rest. But you probably won't even notice this small release when you're sitting in the driver's seat looking out the rear window. (And if you don't believe me here, have someone else start your own car first thing in the morning and stand right behind the tailpipe. Even if it doesn't burn oil between oil changes, you will probably see a small amount of smoke being emitted.) The type of smoke I'm talking about here is a billowing of smoke that continues to circulate behind the car long after the car has been started.

If the billowing smoke is blue (the color of burning oil), the car is burning oil and should be avoided. If you run the tip of your finger inside the exhaust system's tailpipe and it becomes greasy from accumulated oil, the car definitely has engine problems greater than any you and your pocketbook should attempt to repair. This is even more important today than it has been in the past, because many local areas now have mandatory emissions testing of cars. The burning oil would raise the hydrocarbon gas levels greatly and cause most oil burners to fail their emission inspection. You may feel able to "live with" a car that burns a little oil, but your government may feel differently.

If the billowing smoke is black, then the car is throwing out unburned fuel and has too rich a fuel mixture. This can technically be due to many sources, but here is a practical tip: If the car runs decently but puts out black smoke on acceleration, it has a carburetor or fuel injection problem. Note this problem down for your mechanic to check, and get him to give you an estimate on repair cost. The car may still be a good buy if it runs good otherwise, so don't necessarily cross it off your list. But if the car runs poorly (shaking, hesitating on acceleration, or having an engine that makes unusual noises), the problem is often a major engine problem that you should avoid having on your own hands. ALWAYS USE COMMON SENSE- IF A CAR SMOKES AND RUNS POORLY, LOOK SOMEWHERE ELSE. The car in all probability has major problems and you would be wise to invest your time and money in a better car. Why turn someone else's obvious problem into your own headache?

If the billowing smoke is white, the car is burning up the water/antifreeze coolant from its own cooling system; exactly the same as a boiling tea kettle steaming out of its spout. The only exception to this rule occurs when the temperature is very cool outside and the humidity is very high. This white exhaust smoke occurs when it's cold outside and the dew point is low. What you are seeing is the heat of the engine reacting with the moisture in the cool air. It's the same thing that occurs when you can see your breath steaming out of your own mouth in very cold weather. Only it happens to a car in even warmer weather because its exhaust temperature is much higher than your breath (even if you have been eating chili peppers). If it is cool and damp outside, the white smoke coming out of the car will stop as soon as the car has warmed up. It does not mean that there is anything wrong with the car, just as your steaming breath doesn't mean your own head has blown a gasket. But if it is very cold outside, the smoke will not ever stop (at least until spring thaw). If it's cold outside and the car will not stop smoking white, just look at the other cars driving in this cold weather. If they are all billowing out white smoke, it's just the cold weather. You just need to make a note for your mechanic to check out this possible coolant burning in an indoor garage if it is this cold outside. But if it is not this cold outside, and the car keeps billowing out white smoke, the engine has some serious problems and the car should be avoided. A serious engine problem is the number one reason for people to give up on an old car and to start searching for another. So keep your eyes peeled on the exhaust tailpipe for the first five minutes of running while you check the next items.

Once the engine has started up, let it idle in park (or neutral if a standard transmission) for a few minutes. Get out of the car and open the hood. Listen for any strange noises, like clicking sounds or knocking sounds. Rev the engine up and listen again for strange sounds. If the engine has a sound that increases in frequency when the engine is revved up, it may have valve, piston, or bearing damage. These are very expensive engine repairs and should be avoided at all cost. But if the car runs good, these noises may only be symptomatic of relatively minor problems such as clicking electronic fuel injectors or worn engine hydraulic lifters. This is why I must keep stressing the importance of using a professional mechanic to do the final checks on the car. A trained ear with years of experience (and the help of a stethoscope) can tell in just a few seconds whether the knocking sound is a bad piston or just a clicking injector. But during your own personal checking out of the car, keep this advice in mind: IF THE CAR MAKES ODD NOISES AND RUNS POORLY, MOVE ON TO THE NEXT CAR.

If the car runs decently and makes noises, write this down in your notebook and personally show your mechanic what noises you are wondering about. I have seen some of my own customers get fantastic deals on cars that made strange noises but ran ok. As an example, Kelly once brought me a car to check out that was just the model and make she was looking for. It was even the color red she loved. But the engine was making an annoying clicking sound. As the car was only three years old, it shouldn't have been making such a loud noise. But luckily for Kelly, I had recently serviced the exact same make of car a few weeks before. This particular model contained faulty fuel injectors. A new style of fuel injector had just recently been introduced to replace the old style clicking injectors. And although the cost of replacing the injectors was around five hundred dollars, Kelly still saved thousands of dollars by purchasing the car from an owner who was desperate to sell. The clicking noise had scared off many potential buyers, and allowed Kelly to purchase the car at a very good price. The combination of her own thorough checking and her use of a professional mechanic paid off .

While the car is running at idle, you can perform another easy check for major engine problems. Simply take out a dollar bill (or a piece of your notebook paper) and place it directly behind the exhaust system's tailpipe. If the paper is continually being blown away by the exhaust fumes, the engine is running normally. But if the paper is being occasionally sucked towards the inside of the tailpipe, the engine may have major valve problems. A normally running engine only blows out the gas exhaust system; unlike people who blow both in and out of their gas exhaust system (nose). If a car's exhaust system is sucking in as well as blowing out, take the advice of an old horse trader and look for another mount with a better set of lungs.

The last check for you to make before road testing the car is to look under the car after it has been idling during your previous tests. Look for any pools of liquids settling under the car. Antifreeze is normally a greenish color (although other color dyes are occasionally used) and has a sickening sweetish odor to it. Engine oil is a dark color and has a burnt odor to it. Transmission and power steering fluid has a reddish color to it and has a sweet odor to it. And brake fluid is clear with a sweet odor to it. Do not be concerned at this moment about small leaks, as you will analyze them later in your checks. Be on the lookout for LARGE LEAKS that pour steadily on the ground. Unless you are buying a car for practically nothing, large amounts of fluids pouring out of the car should point your head in the direction of another car (one that can hold its fluids better).

THE ROAD TEST

The first check to do on your road test has nothing to do with moving—it has to do with stopping. Put the car in drive (or neutral if a standard transmission) and press down on the brake pedal hard. Keep pressing for about a minute, and see if the brake pedal remains stationary or steadily falls towards the floor. If the pedal loses pressure and sinks with an automatic transmission in drive, the car will begin to creep forwards. In a standard transmission the pedal will just sink to the floor, and the car will only move if you're on a hill. In the old "golden" days of cardom, this pedal sinking meant the brake system had some leakage in the system. But in today's complex computer driven age of ABS (anti-lock braking system) and nitrogen canister brake boosters (rocketship technology used in some cars to create the POWER in power brakes), a sinking pedal can mean many different things. But all you need to know is that a sinking pedal means a brake problem. Write it down in your notebook and discuss it with your mechanic when he checks out the car. Continue on with your road test, unless the brakes sink very quickly and you feel the car is unsafe to drive. If the car is really giving you that sinking feeling, rise out of the quicksand and look for a more solid car. But don't be disheartened here, because very few people attempt to sell a car with completely unsafe brakes. This little one minute test is just to weed out these few cars and to give you a little peace of mind for your road test.

If the car has an automatic transmission, put your foot on the brake pedal and shift the transmission from neutral to drive and from drive to neutral a few times. Do the same shifting from neutral to reverse. Listen for any clunking or grinding sounds, as they indicate a problem in the transmission, the rear end, or the drive shafts. If you're looking at a standard transmission car, do the same test by slowly putting the car in first gear and listening for odd noises when you pick up the clutch. Then do the same test in reverse gear. Write down odd noises you hear (if any) in your notebook.

Now you can begin actually driving the car in traffic (finally!). Plan on driving the car a good twenty to thirty minutes in order to get a good feel of the car itself and what problems it may have. You spend hundreds (if not thousands) of hours riding in a car each and every year, so see this thirty minutes as a very tiny slice of an enormous pie. Drive in stop-and-go city traffic, drive at highway speeds, drive on bumpy roads, and drive on smooth curvy roads. If the car is low on gas (if it is on a car lot that much is guaranteed), go to the nearest gas station and put a couple dollars of gas in the tank. Don't let the seller's excuse of the car being low on gas shorten your test.

While driving the car, you must again keep a little philosophy in the back of your mind. During your drive, you want to get an overall picture of the car, while at the same time you want to check out specific parts of the car. This might sound too complex, but it's not really any different from what you normally do while driving a car. Just think about all the different things going on in your head when you're going for a "normal" trip in your car. You might be controlling (or at least attempting to control) your kids in the back seat, while simultaneously drinking a cup of coffee, listening to your favorite song on the radio, thinking about a dinner party you're planning for Saturday, and wondering whether those wrinkles you see on your face in the rear view mirror are as serious as they look. Compared to the complexity of everyday "normal" driving, taking a solitary road test may even be a pleasure. All you need to concentrate on is the car—whether it is running smoothly and whether all its various parts function or not. If only the rest of our lives were so simple!

Checking the car's heating/air conditioning systems while road testing.

Depending upon the weather and how your car is equipped, turn on the heater or the air conditioner. Try all the fan speed settings to make sure they function correctly. If you are testing an air conditioned car, leave the ac on during your whole trip. This serves the dual purpose of making sure the ac works over an extended period of time, and helps to check the car's cooling system for possible overheating problems. Running an air conditioner puts a heavy load on a car's cooling system,

28

and will make any cooling system problems show up during a thirty minute drive. If the heat doesn't seem warm enough, or the air conditioning doesn't seem cool enough, make a note of this for your mechanic to check.

Checking the car's cooling system while road testing.

Returning to the car's cooling system, you must pay careful attention to its functioning. Most cars today have temperature gauges on them, and this gauge can tell you quite a bit about the car. If your chosen auto does not have a gauge, you must be very careful and rigorously check the car for signs of overheating. And if the car has a temperature gauge that isn't working, be even more suspicious. A very old trick that sellers use in cars with overheating problems is to unplug the wire to the temperature gauge. If your chosen car has a non-functioning temperature gauge, be sure to have your mechanic check the cooling system thoroughly.

Overheating problems in a car can be as simple as a three dollar thermostat, or as complicated as an engine burning itself out. And the problem here (as any truly honest mechanic will readily admit) is that no one can be sure of why this particular car overheats until it has been physically repaired and given a good road test. You may see a blown radiator hose spewing out hot antifreeze, but that may not be the true underlying problem. The engine might be burning out and the extra heat it creates may have finally burst an old hose. The interplay between a car's engine and it's cooling system is very complicated and often will leave even a good mechanic scratching his head in bewilderment. So always keep this advice in the back of your head: IF THE CAR OVERHEATS WHILE YOU ARE ROAD TESTING IT, LOOK FOR ANOTHER CAR. Find one that can keep its cool better.

Discovering if the car overheats while road testing the car is a very simple affair. In cars with working temperature gauges simply watch the gauge (if the gauge always stays at the bottom, or if it shoots up to the very top immediately when the car is started, the temperature gauge is not working). If it slowly moves up to a given position and then basically stays there, the cooling system is working normally. The actual position of the gauge varies from car to car: some cars normally run at halfway between cold and hot, some run three quarters, and so on. But as long as the gauge is not extremely close to the Hot (or even past Hot) the car is not overheating. Most cars have minor fluctuations in their running temperatures: the temperature may move up or down some as the electronic cooling fans kick on and off, or as the car is driven at higher speeds and the wind cools the radiator better. What you are looking for here is a temperature gauge that stays at a relatively stable position (as long as that position is not over the Hot). If your chosen car remains at this stable position during your road test, it is a very good sign. For you have discovered that both the cooling system and the engine itself are in solid shape.

If your chosen car does not have a temperature gauge, or if the gauge is inoperative, you can still determine if the car is overheating (although not to such a fine degree as a gauge will allow). If the car's overheat light starts flashing or remains lit during your drive, it is obvious that the car is getting too hot. But just as with cars with temperature gauges, this warning light may be broken or may have been disconnected. So keep your eyes, ears, and nose on the watch for telltale signs of engine overheating:

1. Watch for steam or fluids coming out from under the hood during the entire road test.

2. Listen for bubbling noises, or hissing noises coming out from under the hood while driving at low speeds.

3. Keep your nose sniffing for any burning smells coming from under the hood. Here you may discover the hot smell of the engine overheating itself, or the hot sweet smell of coolant bubbling out.

When you are almost finished with your road test, stop the car and open up the hood. Look, listen, and smell for any of the above. If the car is truly overheating, you will discover one or more of the following: A.Coolant pouring on the ground. B. Steam rising up out of the engine or radiator. C. A thumping noise coming from the radiator itself or its rubber hoses. The coolant inside is boiling and will often make a very distinctive thumping noise. Sometimes this thumping is so strong that you can actually see the radiator hoses jerk with each thump.
D. A strong sweet odor of boiling antifreeze.

If you have discovered obvious major problems with the car's cooling system, take my previous advice and look for another car that isn't so hot under the collar. But if you have only discovered minor problems (such as small leakage or cracked fan belts), just write them down so your mechanic can check them out further.

Checking out the car's drive train while road testing.

While driving the car in stop-and-go traffic and at highway speeds, get a feel of how the car is running and listen for any odd noises. See how the transmission is shifting when in stop-and-go traffic. Is it smoothly engaging from one gear to another? Or is it giving you a case of whiplash every time it has to change gears? Since many modern cars are equipped with computer controlled automatic transmissions, their repair can be very complex and VERY EXPENSIVE. The days of a three hundred dollar overhaul for an automatic transmission are long gone—I have seen people pay three thousand dollars for such repairs. Problem automatic transmissions are exactly the same as bad cooling systems. You can never be sure what it will actually cost to repair them until they have been physically worked on and severely road tested. If your chosen car has an automatic transmission that has severe shifting problems, go on to the next car. If you are really in love with the car, tell the seller to have the transmission repaired and road test it again after the repairs are completed. I have seen some of my own customers purchase cars that gave them years of good service this way. As long as you road test the car seriously after the transmission has been repaired (a good half hour of driving in mixed conditions), you can be sure the car is fine.

If your chosen car is a standard transmission, also check the transmission in stop-and-go traffic and on the highway. Accelerate hard in first gear, to see if the clutch is slipping. Then accelerate hard in every other gear, to check for grinding noises and to further check for clutch slippage. If the clutch is slipping, the engine itself will begin to run faster, but the car will not accelerate very quickly. This is because the engine is connected to the transmission via the clutch. If the clutch is worn-out, this connection begins to slip as pressure builds up on it. The car will not accelerate correctly when you step hard on the pedal. Although the car runs fine at a steady speed, it will not accelerate correctly when you put your foot to the floor. But do not be disheartened here, because the cost of a clutch job for most cars is only a few hundred dollars (unless you happen to be looking at an exotic sports car where clutches can routinely reach fifteen hundred dollars). If you feel the clutch is slipping, write it down and discuss repair costs with your mechanic.

While driving the car, listen for any odd noises coming from the front of the car. Most cars today are front wheel drive vehicles, so you should listen carefully to front end noises. Both the transmission/differential gear box and the drive shafts are in the front of the car. If they are making loud noises, very expensive repairs may be needed. A very common problem that occurs in front wheel drive cars is that of drive shaft CV (constant velocity) joint damage. To check for this, simply make a U turn to the left, and then make a U turn to the right. If you hear a clicking sound when turning in either direction, there is a CV joint problem. But as loud as it may sound, it is not a major problem. In most cars it would only cost a few hundred dollars to repair. If you hear any questionable noises coming from the drive train, write them down for further discussion with your mechanic.

If your chosen car is a rear wheel drive car, you need to listen for the same noises. They will just be coming from different locations. Most rear wheel drive cars have the transmission in the front of the car, the drive shaft in the middle, and the differential gear box in the rear. (A very few sports cars have the engine in the middle or the rear of the car, with the transmission/differential in the rear.) Listen closely for any suspect noises and try to pinpoint their location. Even if you have no idea what these noises mean, tell your mechanic about them when he checks out the car.

When checking out cars for my own customers, I often go riding with them to discover the source of a noise that bothers them. I have stuck my upper torso out the passenger window like a drooling hound in the wind, as I tried to pinpoint grinding sounds. I have even ridden inside the darkness of a trunk to discover the source of rear end clunking. So I understand that you may not be able to pinpoint the exact location of a particular noise and drive the car at the same time. But you can easily hear strange noises and show them to your mechanic. Unless, of course, the car decides to stop making the noise as soon as it gets within ten feet of a mechanic. From my own professional experience, this old cliche is very often true. But don't be disheartened if it happens to you, because any truly serious problem in a car will not quiet down. Minor problems which are just beginning to surface will often create noises that come and go as they please. But major problems create noises that no man with greasy fingernails and shiny tools can scare away. These noises are permanent fixtures of a car that needs some repairing. And a good mechanic can tell you what such repairing will cost. So KEEP YOUR EARS OPEN DURING YOUR ROAD TEST.

Checking the suspension while road testing.

During your half hour road test, attempt to find roads that are bumpy, roads that are curvy, and highway-style roads that are straight and smooth. You can use them to test the suspension system of the car as follows:

1. On bumpy roads, check to see if the car is bottoming out when you hit bumps. If the car is bottoming out, you will hear banging noises from around the wheels as worn suspension parts hit each other. You will also feel the car's steering wheel getting harder to control. The car may veer to one side or the other.

2. On curvy roads, see if the car handles curves smoothly. Many modern day front wheel drive cars will understeer in corners when the suspension system is faulty. Understeering is when you turn the steering wheel but the car itself wants to follow its previous path and not turn correctly. If the car just doesn't "feel right" during cornering, make a note of this for your mechanic to check out.

3. On straight sections of road where you can drive at highway speeds, see if the steering wheel shakes or pulls to one side. If the steering wheel shakes at all, there is a suspension or tire problem. If the car pulls to one side noticeably, there is a suspension problem (but here you must realize that most roads are graded to the right for rain drainage, and many normal cars will drift slightly to the right if the steering wheel is let go).

After you have driven the car on these three tests, stop the car with the engine running. Roll down the driver's window and get out of the car. While you are watching the driver's side front tire, slowly move the steering wheel back and forth. If you have to turn the steering wheel inches before the wheel begins to move, there are worn-out suspension parts. Normally this will show up during your driving, but sometimes the weight of the car will mask problems that are not yet serious.

Checking the brakes while road testing.
All during your road test, get a good feel for the car's brakes. Are they stopping the car easily? Do they make loud grinding noises when you step on the pedal hard? Do they pull to the left or the right when applied vigorously? Although brake repairs are not usually major expenses in cars, the brake system is the most important safety feature in a car. You should ensure that it is functioning correctly.

If your chosen model has ABS brakes (anti-locking brake system), brake system repairs are often VERY expensive. If you don't know whether the car has ABS or not, look for an ABS symbol on the car. Most cars with ABS will have a symbol advertising this fact, as it is an expensive add-on feature. But if not, ask the seller whether the car has an anti-lock brake system or not. Then be sure to have your mechanic validate this, as the following illustrates. Ed came over to my shop on a sunny spring day driving a red sports car with the top down. He wanted me to check it out as soon as possible, because his next stop was at the bank to cut a cashier's check for the car. Ed beamed that the car was a real cherry—the seller had told him it was fully loaded and even had ABS brakes. Since it was early in the morning and my other work wasn't due until dinnertime, I started checking Ed's dream mobile out. It turned out the car did not have an ABS braking system. Ed's little cherry was not even a fully-loaded auto, it was a base model sports car. But the car itself was very sound, so Ed purchased it. He ended up with both his dream car and unexpected cash left over in his bank account (after he deducted a tidy sum from his purchase price for the luxury items that the car really didn't have).

To check the emergency brake system, pull up hard on the emergency lever, or push down hard on the emergency pedal (depending upon you car's system). If your car has an automatic transmission, put the car in drive and see if the car moves. If it remains stationary, the emergency system is working. If it creeps forwards, the system needs to be repaired. In a standard transmission auto, do the same test on a hill or other incline with the car in neutral. If the car slides down the incline, the system is defective.

Final checks while road testing.

When you've completed the previous road test checks on your car, gather your thoughts about it as you return to the seller. Does the car handle well over rough terrain? Does it sound normal as you accelerate and brake? Does it seem to be running at a normal temperature? Write down in your notebook ANYTHING that you think is " a bit off ". Don't feel intimidated by a lack of technical knowledge. Just attempt to describe what aspects of the car don't feel, sound, or smell right. When dealing with my own customers, I sincerely want them to give me every possible question they have about the car. I gladly explain to them which noises, sounds, and smells are normal, and which mean repair problems. As a good illustration, late model cars today have non-asbestos brake linings, due to the carcinogenic problems associated with asbestos products. The new brake linings work perfectly well and often last much longer than the asbestos linings. But they have one major drawback—a tendency to make squealing and grinding noises when the brakes are applied. For many late model cars, this occasional squealing is perfectly normal. But if you hear these noises in your chosen auto, you should mention it to your mechanic. If it is just normal non-asbestos noise, you will have learned something that will be of benefit to you when owning the car (i.e. you will not be taken advantage of by a dishonest brake repair shop that tells you a brake job is immediately needed). And if the noise is really serious, your check-out mechanic can show you what repairs are actually needed. Either way, you win, AS LONG AS YOU WRITE DOWN EVERYTHING YOU HAVE A QUESTION ABOUT.

When you have returned the car back to its original location, make some final checks. Leave the car running and again look under the car for just a minute. See if you can notice any liquids dripping under the car, as your road test may have brought out leaks that had been previously hidden. And even if the liquid isn't dripping to the ground but is just making parts of the car wet, write any discoveries down. Then turn on every electrical appliance the car has—headlights, parking lights, radio, cd player, windshield wipers, windshield squirters, turn signals, and so on. To ensure that all the windows are functioning correctly, roll each one up and down, ESPECIALLY if the car has electric windows (a notorious used car problem).

Next, check all the government regulation stickers the car has on it, to make sure they have not yet expired. Check the registration sticker, the inspection sticker, and the anti-pollution smog control sticker (if applicable). The stickers in themselves are not that important, although expired stickers can turn into major nuisances (when dealing with bureaucrats, molehills always seem to reach Himalayan heights almost instantly as you reach that little window at the end of the line). More importantly, out of date stickers can be symptomatic of problems the car may have. As an example, the car may have a faulty emergency brake that will not pass the yearly safety inspection. You may not have noticed this while road testing the car, but the safety inspector probably will when you go to get the car inspected. Expired stickers in a car can also be illustrative of overall poor maintenance by the previous owner. If the stickers were allowed to expire, maybe the owner let regular oil changes and maintenance "slide" also. Look at the date on the stickers to see if they all have been done on the same day (or only a few days apart). If they have, be very suspicious of the car's being in a wreck or other catastrophe which sidelined the car for a good length of time. The stickers would have expired while the car was not being driven, and would all have to be replaced when the car returned to the road. Normally, the stickers would come due at different dates on a more or less random probability. But if the car had problems that kept it undriveable for very long, the sticker dates will tend to group together. Close grouping of sticker dates does not prove anything by itself, but it should make you look at the car somewhat closer for possible wreck, flood, or fire damage.

Look at the tires to see if they're in good shape. If their tread shows strange wear patterns, such as too much inside wear, or cupped wear, write it down for your mechanic to check out further. See if all four tires are the same, or whether there is a mix of different brands and tread designs. Don't attempt to judge whether they're full of air or not, unless you have a tire pressure gauge handy. With today's modern low profile radial tires, it's very hard to tell if they're low. Many times I've looked at my own car's tires with that sinking feeling of a developing flat, only to have my pressure gauge make a liar out of my eyes. And whatever else you may wish to do, please don't kick the tires, unless you're in a very satirical mood.

Glance at the speedometer and try to assess if the figure is true. The numbers should be aligned in a smooth line, and should not look like a crooked smile. Speedometers are not very hard to set back, but they are almost impossible to set back with their numbers aligned smoothly. If you are buying the car from a lot, ask to see the mileage statement. It is a legal document which specifies the car's actual mileage, and gives the previous owner's name and address. (If you are buying a car from an individual, they will have to fill out a mileage statement when you transfer the title, but they will not have one to show you now.) Attempt to contact the previous owner and discover if the mileage is real. Which brings us to another caveat—BEWARE THE OUT OF STATE MILEAGE CERTIFICATE. If the mileage certificate has come from out of state, it may be part of the biggest auto scam in history (or at least since mileage statements have become law). Your chosen car may be a high mileage vehicle which had its speedometer set back, and was then sold one or more times to different "owners". Often these sales are just paper deals, with no real exchange of money for car. These paper deals are used to cover up falsified lower mileage statements, which raise the car's value thousands of dollars. There are plenty of good local cars for sale in most areas, so be very suspicious of the interstate commerce mobile. It may very well take you for a ride you'll soon regret.

If you are purchasing a car from its private owner, attempting to discover the speedometer's validity is more direct. Ask to see various receipts of car maintenance, as they often contain both dates and mileage. Look at a few to see if they contain any contradictions. Check them to ensure that the mileage always goes up with time, and doesn't encounter the fountain of youth during any period. Be highly suspicious

36

of a car with no paperwork at all. All cars need to be maintained; they need tires replaced, they need oil changes, they need brake pads replaced, and so on. As this maintenance often comes with warranties, most people will hold on to their receipts in case of problems. The information contained in them is invaluable for your mileage validation, so ask to see them. If your seller can't come up with the goods, don't necessarily dump the car. But be sure to tell your mechanic about it. Let him do a little mileage private eyeing during his check. I can think of more than one time that I've discovered mileage information lurking in the nooks and crannies of an automobile I was checking out. And sometimes this information made a travesty out of the speedometer's "mileage".

FINALLY, yes, FINALLY, ask to see the car's title paperwork. It contains information which can be useful. It will show the owner's name, and also the previous owner's name if the car has had more than one owner. Unfortunately it is not like a family tree, as a car title only goes back two generations. Everyone knows a one-owner car ranks the highest amongst used cars, but you can only be certain of this fact by looking at the title. If a car's title has your seller's name typed in as owner, but has someone else's name as previous lien holder, it is not a one-owner car. Other than in the sense of being owned by one person at a time. And if the title says RECONDITIONED, it has been previously totalled in a wreck or flood (as I have already discussed). If you're really in an unbelieving mood, you can even check the title's serial number against the car's number (that long number stamped all over the car, but most noticeable just inside the windshield on the driver's side). Don't go running away in terror if the title can't be seen right now, especially if the car is on a lot. They often won't have the title on the premises, and are bonded for fraud, making them unlikely to attempt any illegal title maneuvers. But be VERY SKEPTICAL of a private individual selling a car who can't show you the title. With an individual, the title gives you the following critical information:

1. It tells you if this person actually owns the car and can legally sell it to you (I have actually had customers buy cars with no valid title, much to their eventual regret).

2. It tells you whether this person is selling you their own car, or one that someone else owns. This is one of the oldest tricks in the book, where a person advertises a car for sale in the paper. They pretend they are selling you their own car, but the title would show you it is actually

owned by someone else. In reality these people are part-time used car salesmen (and I do mean men, as I have never seen this scam attempted by a woman).

3. The title shows you if the car really is a one-owner beauty, or whether it has had at least one other owner. If you can't see the title now, be suspicious, but don't let it sour the deal. Only be sure to get a glance at the title paperwork BEFORE MONEY CHANGES HANDS, even if it entails a trip to the seller's lending institution.

C. THE EXTRA APPROACH FOR VERY MECHANICAL PEOPLE

This section contains additional checks which can be performed by those bringing along an assortment of tools, and who are willing to get their hands dirty. First, complete all the checks contained in section B, the approach for everyone else. Then finish your investigation with these checks. The checks themselves are not hard to do, so if anyone is still reading from section B, why not read on if you're curious. Don't let the lack of certain test equipment scare you away. You may discover something that you would wish your check-out mechanic to do with his own tools. And even for you mechanically minded people, take my previous advice and don't go out and purchase special tools and test equipment that you don't already have. Unless money is burning that old proverbial hole in your pocket, let your mechanic use his vast assemblage of tools instead. He has already spent plenty of money on all sorts of specialized equipment and is well acquainted with their use. The small fee you pay for a professional mechanic to check out your car is a very good bargain.

Checking the paint and bodywork.

Take a very close look at the car's paint job with the car sitting in direct sunlight. Look for drips, runs, or uneven layering of paint. Examine closely the paint shade, to ensure the car is one exact color. An old trick is to just paint one half of a car when it's wrecked, because you can only see one side of a car at a time. I don't expect you to drive the car into a hall of mirrors, but look at both sides of the car in direct sunlight for possible shading differences. If the car has been wrecked and repainted only in sections, they will fade differently over time and be quite obvious.

Use your nose. Sniff all around the car, under the car, inside the trunk, under the hood, and inside the passenger compartment. If you notice a fresh paint smell, the car has been recently painted. Then you must attempt to discover what has been painted and how much serious damage has been repaired (or has not been correctly repaired, but just painted over). The odor of fresh paint often remains on repainted cars for weeks, so it can lead you by the nose to the evidence of a fresh wreck.

If you suspect a wreck, look for uneven body panels, misaligned doors and trunks, or wavy uneven paint finish. Get out a magnet and attempt to stick it on questionable areas. If it sticks weaker to these metal areas than it does to other similar metal sections of the car, there is body filler material underneath. If the magnet just falls off to the ground in these areas, the car is a virtual Bondo Mobile, and should be avoided at all cost. A good customer of mine used to own one of these venerable beasts. He had only paid three hundred dollars for the car, so it was more of a joke to him than anything else. One day he was involved in a minor rear-end collision, and half of the car's exterior body work just fell off the car's frame and into the street. As no one was injured, he had a good laugh. But I doubt if you would care to spend your own money on such humorous events, so keep your eyes out for bondo repair work.

To further check the body, jack up the car and brace it with a jack stand. Place your old blanket or towel under the car and have a good look. See if there are any obvious signs of wreckage; look for bent frame sections, bent suspension parts, and fuel tanks with large dents in them. Keep a close eye out for fresh undercoating spray, as I've previously discussed. There is absolutely no reason for a used car to have fresh undercoating on it. It is used only to hide body damage in a car, or to cover up rust. If you notice fresh undercoating, look for possible collision damage in the same area. Even if you don't see obvious signs of bent or buckled parts, scrape a few random samples of the undercoating off with a knife or screwdriver end. Look for pieces of rust mixed in with the undercoating. If you discover rust, think about buying another car, as the floorboards of this one are beginning to rust out. And the rest of the car's body is ready to follow suit.

Checking the brake and suspension systems.

As long as you already have the car jacked up, you might as well check the car's braking and suspension systems next. The brakes you can check individually, by spinning the tires and seeing how freely the tire spins. As we definitely don't live in a frictionless world (in more ways than one), no wheel is going to spin freely forever. As many cars today have front wheel drive, the drive axles alone will quickly slow down wheel rotation. What you are looking for here is a relatively free spinning wheel, one that is not hard to begin spinning, and one that does not immediately stop spinning once you stop pushing. You need to have the car's transmission in neutral, and have either the front or rear tires jacked off the ground. Compare the spinning ability of one side to the other; either compare the left front with the right front, or compare the left rear with the right rear. These tires should match each other in their spinning ability, as each is a matched pair. They use the same style brakes, they have the same suspension system, and they have the same drive train section attached to them. If one side spins much slower than the other, something is wrong with the car's brakes or suspension system. Make a note of this excessive dragging and have your mechanic check it out.

With the wheels up in the air, grab a tire with your left hand at the nine o'clock position and your right hand at the three o'clock position. Push in with your left hand and pull out with your right hand, twisting the tire to the left. Then push in with your right hand and pull out with your left hand, twisting the tire to the right. Do this back and forth a few times. See if you notice any loose play in the wheel. Then repeat this entire test with your hands on the tire at six o'clock and twelve o'clock positions. If the car has suspension problems you will notice loose play and hear a low clunking noise. This could mean tie rod problems, or wheel bearing problems, or ball joint problems. But you don't need to uncover the source of this freeplay, just tell it to your mechanic and let his expertise discover its source. Modern day suspension systems have gone a long way from their horse and buggy forbearers. Even a good general mechanic occasionally needs help diagnosing suspension problems. Performing the previous test on all four wheels will tell you whether such a diagnosis is needed.

The next part of the suspension system to check while the car is up in the air is the steering. With a non-power steering car, look at the steering gear box and see if it's leaking grease. Then examine the various tie rods and ball joints for broken or completely missing seals. As most cars today have power steering, examine the power steering hoses for leakage. Follow them from the power steering pump to the steering rack itself. Look at both ends of the steering rack, to see if the boots are not cracked or ripped open. Even if the boots seem ok, give them a good squeeze and see if any power steering fluid seeps out. If it does, the rack is beginning to leak. Power steering racks are relatively expensive to both purchase and install, so make a careful check here. A leaking rack is not a reason to give up on a car, but it definitely lowers the price you should pay for it.

The last section of the suspension system to check is the shock absorbing system. Most modern cars have expensive MacPherson strut type shock absorbing systems, and they are costly to repair. Look at each individual strut (or shock) with your flashlight. Pull any rubber or plastic shield off to the side with a long screwdriver. See if any leakage is occurring around the shaft seals. They should be completely dry; any trace of oil indicates leakage.

If you're feeling in a rather energetic mood, you can remove all the tires and hubs to visually inspect the brake system. See if the brake linings are still relatively thick, or whether they have worn down thinner than a dime and need immediate attention. Look for excessive amounts of rust on the brake system, as this is a bad omen. Either the car has been flooded over the wheels, or the car has been sitting around for a long time without being driven. The steel used in braking system rotors and drums is regular iron-based steel. It will rust when covered with water, or when left undriven for long periods of time. The heat and friction of normal driving burns this rust off when the brakes are applied. But if the car has not been driven for a long time, the rust build-up will be strong and resistant to this burning off. You will easily be able to notice it, especially on the rotors and drums. And if the car has been flooded out, the parts of the braking system that do not rub on the rotors or drums will remain coated with rust forever.

While you're examining for rust, also look for any leakage around the brake system. See if the calipers are damp, or if the wheel cylinders are dripping. If you notice any leaks, wipe them with a rag and take a sniff. If it smells like brake fluid, there's a definite brake leak. But it might be an axle leak and have that pungent gear box oil odor, so be sure to discover what type of fluid leak the car really has.

Checking the car's transmission and drive train.

While the car is still up in the air, take a look at the transmission and its attached drive train. Look for any signs of fluid leakage coming from the transmission, paying special attention to the front main seal, the rear main seal, and both side drive shaft seals (if the car has one drive shaft for each wheel). In a front wheel drive car, or one without a solid drive axle, look carefully at the drive shafts. Examine both constant velocity joints, one at each end of the shaft. Look for cracks or open rips; squeeze the boots to see if any grease leaks out. If the joints are damaged, you would have heard them clacking when making U turns during your road test. But a torn boot will soon cause CV joint damage, so keep your eyes alert for rips and thrown grease around the joint. In cars with a solid drive axle, examine the universal joints at both ends of the driveshaft (and possibly a third carrier bearing joint in the middle of the driveshaft). With the drive wheels jacked off the ground, rotate the driveshaft back and forth slightly. See if any play exists in the universal joints. Then go back to the differential gear box and check it for leaks. In most front wheel drive vehicles, the differential is built into the transmission and they share a common oil supply. But in most rear wheel drive cars the differential is separate, and it needs to be checked by itself. A very few cars (such as Saabs) have a dipstick to check the gear oil, and they are easily checked for proper oil level. Most cars just have a bolt situated midway on the differential for checking oil level. You merely remove the bolt to check fluid level. If the fluid leaks out, or if you can stick your pinkie finger in the hole and touch the fluid, the level is fine. Don't be too worried if you can't find the differential fluid level check bolt, as many are hidden away in rather odd locations and can be very difficult to remove. Just make a note to have your mechanic check it out and show you where it's located.

Checking the car's exhaust system

Before you put the car's wheels back on the ground where they belong, you may as well physically check out the exhaust system. Start up the engine and place a rag over the exhaust tail pipe. Listen for any exhaust leaks occurring under the car. Then crawl under the car and take a closer look. If you suspect any leaks, put your hands close to the area in question and feel for exhaust pulsing. After you've done this, turn the engine off and pick up a small hammer. Tap liberally all around the exhaust system, from the header pipe to the tail pipe. See if the pipes sound solid, or have bits of rust falling off every time you tap. Pay special attention to the catalytic converters, as they can be very expensive to replace.

Take a good general look at the exhaust system to see if anything looks odd. Exhaust systems consist only of metal pipes, mufflers, catalytic converters, and muffler clamps. If you notice different materials, such as stainless steel radiator clamps or fiberglass matting, inspect these closely. An old exhaust trick is to wrap holes up with fiberglass matting or sheet metal, and then tightening radiator clamps over this patch. Look closely around the exhaust system for threaded holes that have no bolts in them; these holes may be the remnants of heat shields which have been removed. Again, if you feel the exhaust system has any suspicious parts, discuss it with your mechanic.

42

Inspecting the car's fluids.

Put the car's wheels back on the ground and park the car on a level surface. Make sure that the car is on flat ground, and not tilting side to side or back to front. It may sound ridiculous, but I have had more than a handful of customers who came to me with grave fears about their car's health. They told me their cars were burning tons of oil, and were afraid the engines were giving out. When they had checked the engine oil, the dipstick showed no trace of oil at all. But when I checked the oil on a level surface, the cars showed to be only half a quart low. They had all checked their oil on an a slanted surface, and unfortunately the slant was away from the dipstick hole. So the cars appeared to be totally out of oil. Needless to say, they were overjoyed with my findings. You don't want to cross off a perfectly good used car mistakenly, so just keep your car "on the level" during fluid inspection.

First, if you have an automatic, check the transmission fluid with the car running in park. The fluid should be between the full and the low line when the car has already been warmed up. The difference between the full line and the low line in most cars is only one pint, so the level doesn't have to be exactly on the full line. Most automatic transmissions hold twelve or more pints of transmission fluid. The heating up and cooling down of this fluid creates expansions and contractions which will make the dipstick reading vacillate somewhat. Just be sure it reads between the full and the low. If the level reads too low or too high, you might want to recheck the transmission for possible leaks. An under-filled transmission usually points to a transmission leak somewhere, and so does an overfilled transmission. Putting the correct amount of automatic transmission fluid in a car is not a simple process. Fluid has to be added with the engine running in park. Then the car has to be driven until it has shifted into all gears (including reverse). Finally, the car has to be rechecked while running in park on a flat surface. Many people accidentally overfill a leaking transmission by not carefully following these procedures. Therefore an overfull transmission is very often symptomatic of fluid leakage. And even if an overfull transmission doesn't show any leaks yet, it will begin to leak in the future if the excess fluid isn't removed. Overfilling an automatic transmission creates too much pressure inside and will eventually blow out seals and cause leakage.

After checking the fluid level, take a good close look at the fluid itself. Wipe the dipstick perfectly clean, and recheck the fluid level. The fluid should be a clean, red color. It should not be dark with specks of dirt in solution, and it positively should not be black. It should smell sweetish like new transmission fluid (take a whiff of new transmission fluid for comparison), and should not have a burnt odor. Lastly, it should definitely not be foamy or have globs of clear liquid floating inside, because this means the transmission has been flooded with water. A contaminated automatic transmission will soon have major transmission difficulties, if it does not already have them. If you suspect contamination, make sure to discuss this with your mechanic.

In a few standard transmission cars, you can check the fluid level by dipstick. The car doesn't need to be running, you just check the level like engine oil. But to check the level in most standard transmissions you need to remove the level checking bolt. This bolt is on the side of the transmission, and may be hard to both find and remove. If you can discover it, remove the bolt and see if the level is full. A full standard transmission will either begin dripping fluid when the bolt is removed, or will have a fluid level close to the hole. Stick your little finger in the hole; if the end of your pinkie gets oily, the transmission is full. The fluid in a standard transmission is not as critical to the transmission's operation as it is in an automatic transmission. It serves to lubricate the gears and helps to cool them down; it doesn't perform major shifting operations like the fluid in an automatic. You want to look for foaming, globular evidence of water contamination, but the actual color of the fluid is not that important. I have personally seen standard transmission cars that have driven over one hundred thousand miles with the original transmission fluid in them. Their transmissions worked perfectly fine, which would be very unlikely if the cars had been automatics.

Check the engine oil after the engine has been turned off a couple minutes. The oil should be close to the full mark on the dipstick, and it shouldn't be jet black. The actual color of the oil can vary immensely, due to the various base oils and additives that different manufactures use. But it shouldn't be black, with only two exceptions: 1. The car is a diesel, where the oil will be stained black within two minutes of having an oil change. (This illustrates the importance of seeing maintenance papers for a used diesel, because there is no other way of proving proper oil change intervals.) 2. The car's oil includes a graphite additive, which stains the oil black. Graphite additives have been mainly replaced by clear mixtures (mainly because of their negative color image) such as Teflon, so this is very uncommon today.

As with transmission fluid, inspect the engine oil for possible water contamination. Water in a car's engine oil is a more common problem than water in automatic transmissions, and it is an even more costly problem. Water in engine oil comes from two sources, and both of them are bad. Either the car was flooded-out, or the water in the car's cooling system is somehow leaking inside the engine. Once water gets inside an engine, it destroys crucial metal parts (such as bearings and rings) and will soon cause the engine to self-destruct. If the car was flooded, immediately changing the oil and flushing out the system can prevent this damage. But this would be of little use in the car you're checking out now, because you have no idea how long ago the water spilled into the oil. And if the water is mixed in the oil because of mechanical leakage occurring inside the engine, the car already has grave problems. NEVER BUY A CAR WITH WATER MIXED IN WITH ENGINE OIL, unless you are purchasing it dirt cheap and plan on installing another engine (or plan on COMPLETELY rebuilding the old engine).

As the old saying goes, oil and water don't mix. This makes it very easy for you to spot water that has entered the crankcase. If the car has sat for a long time, the oil will float to the top of the engine and the water will sink to the bottom. A dipstick that shows an extremely overfilled crankcase, with the oil level way over the full line, is often a signal of water in the oil. The oil is floating above the water, and it looks as if the crankcase contains an overabundance of oil. Actually, the engine has the correct amount of oil, but also has a quart or more of water included. The water increases the volume of liquid inside the crankcase, but due to its higher density the water level usually remains below the dipstick. You would not see the water, unless you opened up the oil drain plug and let the water run out. Only there is an easier way to check out suspected water in the crankcase. When the engine is run for even a few minutes, the water and oil will be churned together by the oil pump. A yellowish, foaming combination of oil and water will result. This gloppy mess is very easy to discover, either on the dipstick or covering the bottom of the engine oil filler cap. If you discover water in the engine oil, DO NOT BUY THE CAR. Even if the seller tells you the engine only needs the head gasket replaced, and offers to knock a few hundred off the price. No one has X-ray eyes and knows what is truly wrong inside an engine. A professional mechanic can perform many complicated tests on an engine and get a reasonable idea, but it is still only an educated guess. The only real way to discover why there is water in the crankcase is to remove the engine from the car and COMPLETELY dismantle it. You should not want to get involved in this very expensive process.

The next fluid to check is the radiator coolant. First, make sure the coolant is not too hot by cracking the radiator cap to its first notch. If steam or hot coolant doesn't escape, open the cap fully and remove it. Inspect the coolant for signs of corrosion, draw some out of the radiator (or the overflow canister) and put it in a glass or cup. Coolant comes in many colors (red, blue, and green are the most common) and sometimes people inadvertently mix different brands to create new shades. The actual color is not important, what you are looking for is contaminated antifreeze. See if you notice flecks of corrosion floating in the coolant, and definitely look for floating globules of oil. Oil in the coolant system is the same as coolant in the engine crankcase oil—a sign to move on to the next car.

Then attempt to look down inside the radiator to inspect its interior for possible corrosion build-up. In many cars, shining a flashlight down the radiator cap hole will work. Some cars have their radiator cap located on a tank away from the actual radiator, so you won't be able to do this. If you are extremely interested in checking the radiator core on this type of cooling system, you can remove the upper radiator hose and peer inside. Look for corrosion and scale that covers the interior cooling tubes. See if you can flake any scale off with a long flat-headed screwdriver; if the answer is yes, the radiator will soon cause overheating problems (assuming it doesn't already). The only way to solve heavy scaling in a radiator is to replace it with a new one, or to have a radiator shop remove it from the car and physically rod out the scale in an acid bath. You might opt out for the second option in a car you already own, but my advice for a used car purchase would be to deduct the price of a new radiator (plus labor) from your offer.

If you own a small hand-held radiator pressure tester, attach it to the radiator cap hole and pump it up. Don't go out and purchase one just for this test, as your mechanic certainly has one. However, if you plan on using a tester for diagnosing and possibly repairing your own car's cooling system, there are many non-professional testers available that would suit your purpose. They are not very expensive, and are a very useful tool for home mechanics. Ensure that the tester's cap is sealed tightly by spilling a little dishwashing liquid on it and watching for bubbles. If you notice any, remove the tester and put a dab of dishwashing liquid on the tester's seal. Reattach the tester and pump up the system to around twelve pounds. Then let the tester sit for five minutes, to check for slow leaks in the system. The tester's gauge will drop in pressure if there are any leaks. If this occurs, listen for the noise of escaping air or coolant, and try to pinpoint the source of the leak. But if the pressure leak is very slow, and you are unable to locate the source, be sure to tell your check-out mechanic. A very slow leak that can't be seen may be inside the engine, so be sure to have your mechanic discover the whereabouts of any undecipherable slow leaks.

The next fluid to check is the power steering fluid, if your chosen model does not have manual steering. Open the power steering reservoir and see if the level is normal. Take a small sample of the fluid and examine it in a glass or cup. Most power steering fluid is red, but some cars use a mineral oil that is basically clear. Inspect the fluid for impurities—little pieces of material floating in the liquid. As with automatic transmissions, be wary of very dark fluids, and certainly be suspect of black fluid. Modern-day cars have very expensive power steering systems; the small amount of time you will spend checking the power steering system out can save you much grief later. If any problems are discovered, deduct the cost of REPLACEMENT from the car's value. The pressures inside power steering systems are extremely high, and you should not plan on having defective parts repaired. Reseal jobs on power steering pumps and steering racks often do not last even one year. Remanufactured units have a decent track record, but my advice would be to base your repair figure on new units. A broken part which has been repaired rarely has the longevity of a brand new one.

The last fluid to check is the brake and/or clutch fluid. The fluids in both systems are the same, and in some cars (such as BMWs) they even share a common container. Open the cap and look at the fluid—it should be perfectly clear. If possible, take a sample of the fluid and examine it in a glass or cup. Look for any impurities, especially if the fluid is darkened or has turned completely black. Contaminated brake fluid in a car will eventually destroy all the rubber seals in the entire brake system. It is also symptomatic of overall poor automobile maintenance; extremely dirty brake fluid should tell you to take a closer look at other parts of the car to check for correct maintenance. If you suspect contaminated brake fluid, make a note to have your mechanic check the entire brake system over with a fine tooth comb.

In standard transmission cars with hydraulic clutch systems, examine the fluid identically. Although clutch hydraulic repairs are generally not as complex and expensive as brake system repairs, you may as well check the system out. And if your chosen car does have an expensive clutch hydraulic system (such as a Saab or a late model Jeep) which requires removal of the transmission to replace, you should inspect the system thoroughly. The system only consists of two main parts, the clutch master cylinder and the clutch slave cylinder, so it is fairly simple to check. Look directly under the clutch pedal to discover the rod that connects the pedal to the clutch master cylinder. Search for any signs of leaking brake fluid where the rod enters the master cylinder, and notice if any fluid is soaking into the carpet below. Then follow the metal clutch line that emerges out of the master cylinder's other end. It will lead you to the clutch slave cylinder, located somewhere on the car's transmission. Inspect it for leaks in the same manner. If the rubber boot covering of the slave cylinder is accessible, squeeze it to see if any fluid seeps out. Slave cylinders that have just begun to leak will not always be externally leaking, as they often have two levels of seals. If fluid seeps out when you squeeze the external boot, the cylinder is beginning to fail and should be replaced. In standard transmission cars with cable operated clutch systems, merely examine both ends of the cable for frayed or broken strands.

Checking the engine.

Now it's time to check the most important part of the car—the engine. Since the main purpose of your car is to get you from here to there, the power behind this transporting should be examined very closely. With your road test already completed, you should have a good feel about the engine's general condition. You've discovered how the engine idles, how it accelerates on the highway, whether it is smoking out the tailpipe, and whether it makes any odd knocking noises. Now it's time to get out the fine tooth comb and check the engine very closely. The easiest, most revealing test you can perform is to check each spark plug's condition. Remove them one at a time and line them up. See if all the spark plugs have an identical firing color. The color on the firing tip should be light gray to light tan—IT SHOULD NOT BE ANY OF THE FOLLOWING COLORS:

1. A dull, dry black color with fluffy carbon deposits on it. These spark plugs illustrate an engine that is running too rich.

2. A wet, black color with small nodules of burned oil. These spark plugs illustrate an engine that is burning oil.

3. A yellow or tan colored insulator tip. These spark plugs illustrate an engine that is lead fouled. With the phasing out of leaded gasoline this is no longer a major problem in most areas.

4. A glazed yellow or brownish build-up on the electrode and the insulator tip (the white ceramic part in the middle of the spark plug itself). These spark plugs illustrate a fuel related problem; either the fuel

itself is contaminated, or an improper type of fuel or oil additive has been used by the previous owner.

The reading of spark plug colors and wear patterns is indeed an art, so don't attempt to make your own conclusions unless the problem is obvious—such as all the plugs being jet black. If you suspect any problems, be sure to have your mechanic inspect the engine and its spark plugs very closely. Especially if some of the car's plugs are normal looking and some are not. This is often indicative of a bad cylinder (or cylinders) in the engine; but sometimes it could simply be bad spark plug wires causing the plugs to misfire. IF THE SPARK PLUGS ARE NOT ALL ONE UNIFORM COLOR, BE SURE TO TELL YOUR CHECK OUT MECHANIC. And when reinstalling the spark plugs, be sure to put them back in their original cylinder number. You do not want to confuse your mechanic by mixing them up and causing an analytical nightmare.

If you have the equipment, you can take compression readings of the individual cylinders when you've removed the spark plugs. Very inexpensive compression gauges are available at most auto parts stores. The easiest to use are the ones that have rubber tips and are simply pressed tightly against the spark plug hole to check compression pressures. The testers which screw into the spark plug hole are both more expensive and much harder to use. If they are not seated correctly, you will get wildly inaccurate readings from them. And if correctly seated, they are often a lesson in sheer frustration to remove. The old rubber tipped gauges do have a tendency to wear out their tips, but you probably won't be using it hundreds of times like a professional mechanic would. And if the gauge itself isn't long enough to fit your car, you only have to take a trip to the local hardware store to customize it. These gauges are all pipe fitting size; the boys at the hardware store can cheaply thread you a piece of pipe and sell you any fittings for only a few dollars. Just remember to bring the gauge along for them to measure its pipe size (as standardization has never reached the plumbing industry either).

When checking the compression pressures of each cylinder, just push the gauge in the spark plug hole tightly and crank the engine over five or six times. You can remove the coil wire from the distributor if you don't want the engine to start up. But don't worry if your car is one of the newer models with the coil inside the distributor, where you can't remove the wire connection. It doesn't matter if the car starts up while you are checking individual cylinder pressure. With the spark plug removed, that cylinder can't fire and the compression reading will be accurate. As long as the spark plug lead for the cylinder you are checking has been safely moved away from your hands, you are in no danger of being zapped.

The actual pressure readings of individual car motors varies quite a bit, from a low compression engine's normal reading of 140 pounds per square inch to a high compression diesel engine's reading of 550 pounds per square inch. (I would advise those looking at a diesel engine to have a professional mechanic check out compression pressures in any diesel engine. The extremely high operating pressures and very expensive test equipment that is needed for diesel compression checks is something better left to a professional. Accessing the glow plug holes to check diesel compression is very tough on many diesel engines. Improperly removing or reinstalling the glow plugs can often cause expensive engine damage.)

What you are looking for in engine compression readings is consistency. No cylinder's pressure should be more than ten percent lower than any other cylinder. Car engines normally wear some over time, causing the pressure of a used engine to be lower than a new engine. And pressure gauges are not always perfectly calibrated—they are only one hundred percent accurate in relation to their own readings. If your gauge reads one hundred and thirty pounds per square inch for every cylinder, the engine is probably in good shape. But if three cylinders read one hundred and fifty pounds, and one cylinder reads one hundred and twenty pounds, the engine has problems in the low cylinder. If you suspect a compression problem in your car, but the car seems to run ok, discuss this with your mechanic. He had more advanced tools to check out possible problems (such as compression leak down testers and compression balance testers). But if your car runs poorly and shows a compression problem, I would advise looking for another vehicle.

With your flashlight in hand, carefully examine the engine for possible oil leaks. Small problems like leaking valve cover gaskets aren't that big of a deal (unless you are planning on buying an exotic car like a V12 Jaguar where you can easily spend 800 dollars replacing them). What you are looking for are the big problem oil leaks—the front main engine seal, the rear main engine seal, and the head gasket(s) seal:

1. First, find the front main pulley that's bolted on the end of the crankshaft. This is where all the fan belts get their common drive power from. Inspect the area directly behind the pulley for signs of engine oil

seepage, looking at all 360 degrees around the circular seal. A bad front main engine seal will throw mists of oil back on the engine block itself. A completely worn-out seal will drip oil down the middle of the crankcase pan whenever the engine is running.

2. Second, go the the back side of the engine where the engine and the transmission are bolted together. The rear main engine oil seal is located directly above this meeting point of the engine and transmission. You can not access the seal without removing the car's engine or transmission, but you can discover if the seal is leaking. All cars have a small gap (or an actual inspection cover grate) between the engine and transmission. If this area is soaked with engine oil, the seal is probably bad (if the area has transmission fluid on it, the front main seal of the transmission is leaking). Any suspicious leaks should be reported to your mechanic, who can tell you the cost of repair to deduct from the car's selling price.

3. Third, look at the head gasket(s) area of the engine very closely with your flashlight. All cars have one or more head gaskets that seal the engine's heads against the engine's block. Look at the valve cover to find the top of one head, and then go down half a foot or so. The long thin line between the bottom of the head and the top of the block is where the head gasket lives. If you see oil or coolant leaking out of this area, you have a head gasket leak. If the car runs ok and you notice head gasket leakage, have your mechanic give you the cost of replacing the gasket and deduct it from the car's selling price. The head gasket is just beginning to break down, and the engine itself is fine. But if the car does not run well and shows gasket leakage, I'd advise you to look for another car. This engine could have head or block problems which could not be discovered without physically taking the engine apart. If the engine you are checking out has a V configuration or opposing cylinders, be sure to check all the head gaskets closely.

The last engine aspect to check is the overall quietness of the engine's operation. Run the engine at idle and listen for any odd noises—clicks, knocks, or rumblings. Then rev the engine up and see if you notice any new clicks or knocking sounds. If you hear any odd sounds, try to discover if they increase in frequency or in loudness as you rev up the engine. Any questionable noises should be referred to your mechanic, who can use years of experience to decipher the underlying cause. A bad clicking fuel injector can sound very much like a faulty intake valve. The fuel injector replacement may only be a hundred dollars, but a valve job may easily top a thousand. If you happen to own a stethoscope, you can check fuel injector noise out by simply placing the business end on each injector. Compare the sounds, listening for one or more injectors which are significantly louder than the rest. It is exceptionally rare for all the injectors in a car to go bad at the same time. The bad injector(s) will click much louder than the good injector(s). But if you car clicks and it is not fuel injector noise, just give this information to your check out mechanic and let him sort it out. Internal engine sounds require a very experienced ear and some extremely expensive diagnosis equipment to decipher.

Checking the car's electrical system.

The final element to check on the car is its electrical system. Begin with the battery, because any electrical testing equipment you may use can give you wildly inaccurate readings if the battery itself is defective. In a battery with accessible filler holes, open all six holes. See if the metal plates are covered with battery acid in every hole. If the battery is a sealed unit, look at the glowing eye inspection hole and discover if it is within the specifications printed on the battery top. A defective battery can lead to extremely bizarre operating conditions; both for electrical test equipment and the car's actual running itself. I once worked on a car that would not start. The car was a modern electronically fuel injected car, which was very dependent upon proper battery voltage for smooth running. The car's engine would crank over and over, but it would not start up. It's owner thought he had a fuel problem, or an ignition problem. But the only problem I discovered was a bad battery. I checked the battery and it showed low voltage on my meter. When I jumped started the car, the engine immediately began running. The old battery had enough juice to spin the engine over, but not enough to run the various computer driven systems that get the engine to fire up. Although this is a relatively rare problem (as bad batteries will not usually crank the engine over at a relatively normal speed) you should ensure that the battery is in good condition. There are much more subtle problems that can arise in a car's electrical system which can be directly traced to a faulty battery.

If you have any electrical test equipment, such as a voltmeter or ampmeter, hook them up to the car. When testing the battery voltage, hook the meter to the battery and make sure it tests within the good range of your meter. Then start the car up, and see if the voltage range for the alternator is in the good range when the engine is idling. Then turn on every possible accessory—the radio, the bright headlights, the air conditioner or blower fan on high speed, and the windshield wipers. See if the alternator is still testing within the good charging range. If it no longer does, rev the engine up and see if the good charging range is reached. A charging system that shows good voltage at full load (with all the accessories turned on) when the engine is revved up, but low voltage when the engine is just idling is a little weak. It may still function for a long time. I once diagnosed a customer's car as having this exact problem, and discovered she was still driving the car two years later without having made any alternator repairs at all. But if the car's charging system continues to show a low voltage at full load even when the engine is revved up, there is a definite charging system problem.

For those of you without gauges, you can still make a general charging system check. With the engine idling, turn the headlights on at high beam. Rev the engine up, and notice if the headlights go from dim to bright. If they do, the charging system is weak. If the brightness remains constant, turn on all the electrical accessories as previously discussed in the gauge section. Rev up the engine again, and notice if the lights go from dim to bright. This would also indicate a charging system problem. But do not try to further diagnose the problem, let your mechanic discover its roots. And please, DO NOT USE THE OLD CHARGING SYSTEM TEST OF REMOVING THE NEGATIVE BATTERY TERMINAL WHILE THE CAR IS RUNNING, YOU CAN SEVERELY DAMAGE THE CAR'S ELECTRONICS. In the pre-computer age of cars, you could remove the battery's negative terminal while the car was running, as long as it was only for a few seconds. If the car died, the charging system was undercharging, and if the car remained running, the charging system was working. But in the meantime, cars have been "taken over" by complex interconnected computer systems. Many even have computerized alternators. All these computer systems can easily be severely damaged by removing the negative battery terminal while the car is running.

For your final electrical checks, use every electrical device the car contains to ensure their proper operation. Turn the radio or other entertainment device on, notice if the cassettes or cds play correctly. Check each power window for ease of operation, and do the same with a sun roof. Try the heater and the air conditioner at all different speeds. Check electrically operated mirrors, electrically operated seat adjustments, remote control trunks, gas cap cover remote openers, windshield wipers and squirters, and any other device you car may have. It won't take but a few minutes, and it will give you peace of mind knowing that you've finished off a good job correctly.

Chapter 4

HAVING A MECHANIC
CHECK OUT THE CAR

Now that you've performed the various duties of chapter three, you should have a very good feel for your chosen vehicle. Your head and notebook should be full of information (except for those who have taken the absolute minimum approach). You have discovered both the good and bad aspects of the car. (Unless your chosen car has turned out to be a "cream puff" and you haven't found any bad aspects.) You now need to discuss these aspects with a good mechanic. If you have taken the minimum approach, it is of utmost importance that you use a very good mechanic. You'll have to explain that you haven't checked the car out in-depth, and that you want the mechanic to go over the car with a fine tooth comb. You have decided on taking a bigger gamble, and have put most of your eggs in the mechanic's basket. It is very critical for you minimimalists to use an expert, honest mechanic. Certainly, everyone else also wants to use an expert mechanic; but those who have diligently done their own in-depth checking are in a much better position. They are not going to a mechanic with relatively little knowledge of the car. They can give good feedback to the mechanic and greatly facilitate his process of checking the car out.

In this sense, treat your trip to the check-out mechanic exactly the same as a trip to the doctor. Realize that the mechanic is going to spend a limited amount of time checking out your car; the same as a doctor is going to spend a limited amount of time checking out you. If you are able to speed the process up by giving valuable insight into the car's possible problems, you will greatly facilitate matters. Mechanical creations (cars) are much less complex than biological creations (people). Any information you give the mechanic can quickly help him discover any problems that are lurking inside the car. If you feel a mechanic is not listening to what you are telling him, then you are dealing with the wrong mechanic. You need to do exactly the same thing you'd do with a doctor who does not listen—go find another who will listen.

As a mechanic myself, I actually enjoy listening to my customers while checking out cars for purchase. I find checking out cars to be a most enjoyable process. I get to play detective and attempt to locate every little thing that may be wrong with a car. I search for all the little tricks that people have used over the ages to disguise problems. And best of all, I don't have to repair anything (at least not until later, if the car is purchased). After twenty five years of repairing cars, it's quite nice to discover problems and not have to fix them right away. For me, checking out cars is a service that is a great deal of fun.

Those of you who are not finding it easy to discover an honest, expert mechanic may let out a collective moan right now (and those who have found one can give a little sigh). Many good mechanics are out there, just as there are many good doctors. If my previous advice on locating a good mechanic has not yet worked for you, I will give you some tid bits to help you discover one. But before you begin a search for a good check-out mechanic from scratch, give the word of mouth approach one more try. Ask all your friends and associates if they know of a good, honest mechanic. Word of mouth is a very powerful tool when searching for a mechanic. Any mechanic can pay for professional advertising which extolls his great expertise at repairing automobiles— even if he actually has very little real expertise. The advertising company is only interested in being paid for their work, they often have no idea if the mechanic is good or bad. And judging by many of the advertisements themselves, which often contain small disclaimers, they certainly aren't aware of the mechanic's honesty. Many advertisements will state claims similar to the following: "Brake jobs, $49.95." But there will be a small asterisk, which leads to tiny print that says "most cars". Don't be shocked when your car is never included in the most car category. The mechanic is just being dishonest and using the advertisement to "sucker" people into his shop. But no one can pay for word of mouth advertising. It must be earned by a mechanic, and as such it is priceless for both the consumer and the mechanic. The mechanic does not have to waste his money purchasing advertisements, and you do not have to waste your time worrying about the mechanic's abilities. Use all your possible networking ability to discover a good mechanic, because NOTHING beats word of mouth advertising.

Tips On Discovering A Good Mechanic
   In the highly unlikely scenario that you just can't hear about a good mechanic to check out your car, you'll have to discover one yourself. I do mean unlikely, because in this day and age nearly every family owns a car. All cars need to be maintained (or at worst need to be repaired when things go wrong). With the high tech nature of modern cars, this often requires the use of a mechanic. Unless you are living an extremely Spartan loner existence, you are going to know people who have used mechanics. Perhaps you don't believe other people's advice, or maybe you've grown weary of your old mechanic and are looking for a new one. Maybe your old trusted mechanic has (gasp) moved away, or has (moan) retired. Whatever the reason, the following advice should greatly facilitate your search for a good, honest mechanic:

1. Discovering a garage or repair shop itself is a simple task—they are seemingly everywhere. You have to decide if the people inside are worth their salt. This is where the simplicity ends, as you can't just ask them if they are good mechanics and then let them check out your car. Only a total cretin would answer, "No, I'm a terrible mechanic. Take your money to someone who knows what they're doing." You need to understand what a good mechanic should be like. This knowledge does involve a certain amount of personal prejudices, but being a mechanic myself, I feel these opinions can make your search a better one.

2. First, check out the age of the mechanic you're going to be dealing with. A solid middle aged mechanic is a big favorite, but don't dismiss an older mechanic with all those years of experience. My grandfather was a great mechanic in his prime, and was still a very good one in his seventies. Be extremely wary of very young mechanics when having a car checked out. For those thinking I'm being harsh and possibly an old stick-in-the-mud, I do realize that I was once young too. But I did not know one-tenth of the information I now know about cars, and would not have done an excellent job checking out an entire car for purchase. Just like a young doctor fresh out of medical school, I did not have enough hands-on experience of all the possible problems that can crop up. I could have easily missed incipient problems lurking in a used car, not to mention misdiagnosing relatively major problems. Many of the chain repair shops are manned only by young inexperienced mechanics, because their pay level is too low (often bordering on minimum wage). Try to avoid these types of shops when having a car checked out.

3. As ridiculous as it might sound, look at a mechanic's style of dress. A mechanic's lot is often a dirty one, and a true mechanic will look the part. He doesn't need to be covered in grime and filth, but he certainly shouldn't look like Dr. Kildare. I have personally met "mechanics" who dressed up in white lab coats and smoked pipes as an affectation. They were only posing as good mechanics. In reality they had a poor grasp of automotive diagnosis and repair. Quite a few repair shops have these poseurs walking about; they will gladly talk your ear off, but don't bet the ranch on the verity of their information. If you feel you chosen mechanic may be one of these, take a glance at his hands. If they're baby smooth with no calluses, you've got a talker on your hands, not a mechanic.

4. Talk to your prospective mechanic. Do not use someone who talks to you in a condescending manner—not only is it unprofessional, it is also

unnecessary. Modern cars may be technologically complex, with many interrelating computer control networks running the show, but their basic operating principles are the same as an old Model T Ford. All four stroke gasoline (or diesel) engines operate on the same basic level. A fuel/air mixture has to be created. This mixture has to be injected into the engine's cylinders. The mixture then has to be ignited, and the gases resulting from this explosion have to be removed from the cylinder. The actual devices that control this process can be extremely complex when taken as a whole; but each step can be explained to anyone who is interested in understanding how the entire process works. This same logic applies to every part of the car—be it the transmission, the braking system, or any other part that needs to be explained. A mechanic should be able to explain how any part of your car works, and does not need to use complex terminology. When it comes down to discovering what is wrong with a particular system in the car, this discussion can admittedly become very complex. Even mechanics can be intimidated by some intermittently occurring problems that seem to come and go as they please. But a good mechanic should be able to tell you how the car's systems generally work, and how they relate to one another in the total operation of the vehicle.

5. Look around the mechanic's shop and examine its general appearance. See if it's a busy shop, or if you are the only customer in sight. Only here you must act like a detective looking for important clues—don't always accept everything you superficially see as an obvious sign that the shop is full of cars being worked on. As an example, I once knew a very poor mechanic's shop whose parking lot was always full of cars. They were various "junkers" that the owner kept around to lure customers in. These "decoys" did lure quite a few unsuspecting people in, as the shop was on a busy street corner with plenty of potential customers driving by every day. But a knowledgeable person can walk over to these cars and examine them. See if some are missing engines, or have expired inspection stickers, or are covered in dirt and have obviously not been driven for a long time. If there are more than a few of these cars sitting around, odds are they're sitting there as customer decoys.

6. Look at the shop's equipment to see what type of machinery and test equipment the mechanic is using. Remember, a repair shop is not a restaurant kitchen where everything has to be clean and shining. Many frequently used tools and machinery get grimy very quickly in the

automotive repair business. They still serve their purpose well, even though they seem a bit frayed around the edges. I have known a few obsessive/compulsive mechanics who kept their shops immaculately clean with every tool placed on its own special hook with an outline of the tool neatly drawn behind it. These mechanics were not any better than others I'm acquainted with. They were just putting out an image for their customers (an image that the customers often paid dearly for).

When looking at the mechanic's equipment, do not be overly impressed by large diagnosis machines and their huge computer screens. These machines are only helpful diagnosis tools and are only as good as the mechanic using them. Their manufacturers have deliberately designed them for show—they are large, colorful, and look very impressive. But the insides of these machines are often 95% empty space. A small hand held diagnosis computer will do the job just as well, as long as the mechanic understands its operation. I once had a customer show up with a three foot long printout from one of those huge diagnosis computers. He had been to a chain repair shop, and wanted a second opinion before he shelled out five hundred dollars for a new carburetor. The printout was full of exhaust gas analysis percentages and other innumerable, almost mysterious figures. The bottom of the third page had been circled, and it read "needs new carburetor". I took the air cleaner assembly off the top of the carburetor, and took a general look around the carburetor. I quickly discovered that the wire for the electric choke had become disconnected. After plugging the wire back in its socket, the car began to run perfectly. In this particular case, the use of a huge diagnosis computer would have served one of two purposes. It would have been a prop in a scam to "rip off" the customer. Or it would have been a poorly used piece of diagnosis equipment. Either way, the customer would have lost if he had believed the paper he had been originally given. So do not be overly impressed by fancy-looking diagnosis machines. They are very expensive and you can just guess who ends up paying for their cost.

7. Ask the mechanic if he has any types of automotive repair certification—such as air conditioning certification, brake certification, or automatic transmission certification. Certification is only a small part of being a good mechanic, but it is an easy one to check. All automotive certification institutes give paper diplomas or metal signs for the mechanics to post at their shops. Just don't put too much faith in these certificates. The certification tests are often notoriously easy to pass. There is also a world of difference between understanding the

theoretical basis of a car's particular system and being able to correctly repair the actual problems that occur everyday in real cars. As my grandfather/mechanic used to say, "I don't trust those book trained boys. They're all book and no practice."

8. Lastly, if you've gone through this process and feel the mechanic is a good choice, explain a little of your own situation to him. When looking for a truly reliable check-out mechanic, you should be sure to mention that you also need someone to maintain whatever car you eventually purchase. I have personally had a few customers over the years who would have me check out used cars for them to purchase, but who never used me to maintain the cars after purchase. Years later, they would bring me another used car to check out, but I would not see them again for maintenance. I know people can do some very strange things, but this behavior still puzzles me. If they trust me enough to check out their future mode of transportation (literally putting their moving lives in my hands), why don't they trust me to fix them? (Wonders may never cease in this great big world of ours.) I attempt to treat all my customers with the same level of courtesy and professionalism; but you'll probably find quite a few mechanics who aren't so understanding. If they feel you're not going to use them for later maintenance and repair, they may not do a very concise job when checking out a car for you. Considering the relatively small fee that most mechanics charge for checking out a car, part of the cost is written in as future profit in maintaining the car. The mechanic is putting his reputation on the line every time he seriously checks out a car. You should show him you appreciate the service and plan on using him after a good car is checked out and purchased.

The Check-Out Process Itself
   Now that your chosen car has arrived at the mechanic (or the mechanic has arrived at the car, as there are mobile check out mechanics), it's time to ensure the process goes smoothly. Give the mechanic all the information you have already gathered on the various pros and cons of the car. If your notebook is relatively full, let the mechanic use it as a reference while checking out the car. IF YOU HAVE ANY POSSIBLE QUESTIONS OR DOUBTS ABOUT THE CAR, TELL THE MECHANIC NOW. This may sound like an obvious thing to do, but I can think of numerous times that my own customers did not mention problems with a car until after I had already finished checking the car out. This is why your check-out notebook should be

put to good use. Whenever you think of anything that seems "not quite right" about the car, jot it down in your notebook. That way you won't forget to mention it when the mechanic begins to look the car over. I use notepads endlessly when working on cars, jotting down all the information I need as each car is being worked on. Otherwise I'd certainly forget important pieces when I made my trip to the auto parts store.

There are certain critical parts of the car that everyone should have their mechanic check out, as the following explains:

THINGS EVERYONE SHOULD
HAVE THEIR MECHANIC CHECK

1. The General Shape Of The Engine.

Have the mechanic check the engine for odd noises or fluid leakage, and for its general operating condition. Most mechanics will pull out the spark plugs for a good analysis of the engine's worthiness. But if you suspect a problem, or wish to be extremely conservative, you can ask him to perform a compression test on each cylinder. Here you must realize that the mechanic is in a similar position to a doctor. Anyone who has recently had a complete physical examination understands the added time and expense needed for specialized testing. If you wish the mechanic to perform many specialized tests on the car, you should expect to pay for them on an hourly basis. If something particular is bothering you about the car, it's worth paying an extra twenty-five dollars or so to discover if it really is something to worry about. But don't get paranoid and ask him to perform every test with every single piece of equipment he has—it would be extremely expensive and isn't necessary with a good mechanic.

2. The Condition Of The Engine's Timing Belt.

Most modern day cars have a rubber based timing belt that drives the engine's cam shaft(s). This belt is inside the front of the car and can not be seen without removing its various covers. If this belt ever breaks, the engine will immediately stop, which is a big enough problem in itself. But if your car has a racing designed engine with valves and pistons having very close tolerances, a broken timing belt spells DISASTER for the engine. The pistons and valves will hit each other in such an engine when the belt breaks, and will often cause thousands of dollars of damage. This engine design evolved from race car engineering, but it now shows up in different styles of vehicles—many of which you would hardly call race cars. As an example, many mid eighties Honda Civics had such an engine, and you would certainly not view them as race cars.

YOU NEED THREE PIECES OF INFORMATION FROM YOUR MECHANIC ABOUT THESE TIMING BELTS: 1. Have him tell you if your car has a timing belt. Some cars still use metal timing chains and do not have the problems of the more fragile timing belts. 2. If your car does have a timing belt, have your mechanic tell you whether the engine will bend valves and/or pistons if the belt breaks. Many cars, such as most Toyotas, have engines that are not damaged when the timing belts break. It is a much sounder engine design, and it really does not affect performance to any noticeable degree. Unfortunately, there are still quite a few engineers out there gazing down on us all from ivory towers. These racing designed engines continue to be used in everyday transportation cars, and they require very deliberate maintenance scheduling. 3. See if your mechanic can access the timing belt and give you a report on its condition. Many engines have access covers that are easily removed, allowing for timing belt inspection. Timing belt maintenance varies from car to car, but they generally should be replaced every sixty thousand miles. (Your mechanic can give you the figures for your particular vehicle.) With non valve bending engines, this mileage can be pushed upwards with no fear of major problems. But with valve bending engines, it is better to be safe than sorry. If your mechanic has any questions about the timing belt's condition, have the price of replacing the belt deducted from the car's selling price. In most cases this is just a few hundred dollars, unless you're thinking of buying a rather exotic car. The price of changing the timing belts in late model Porsches can exceed fifteen hundred dollars.

3. The Condition Of The Transmission.

You want your mechanic to give you a report on the transmission's overall condition—how it's shifting, whether it's leaking fluid, and if the clutch is slipping (for standard transmissions). Visual inspections and a vigorous road test by the mechanic will give him all the information necessary. But if you noticed anything strange about the transmission during your road test, be sure to tell him. The more information available, the better. As a rather bizarre example, I once met a woman with a very strange transmission problem. A friend had told her about me, and she was extremely frustrated with her car. She had been to various dealerships and had already spent five hundred dollars to no avail. Her car had the same exact problem. When the car was driving over fifty-five miles an hour, and was going up an incline, the car would suddenly quit. At all other times it ran perfectly. The fuel injection system had been worked on, the fuel pump had been replaced, the car had been tuned up—but it would still quit when running fast uphill. Although the car only had one main problem, she had two: 1.The mechanics working on the car were not listening to her (I assume at least some of them didn't believe her story and didn't seriously road test the car.) 2.The mechanics had all looked at the wrong part of the car. It sounded like a transmission problem to me, because computer controlled automatic transmissions are the only part of a car that I have ever seen cause such a problem. I seriously road tested the car, and discovered that the transmission was indeed the problem. But if I had been checking out that particular car for purchase, I might have missed something which was so odd and only occurred in such a limited circumstance. This is where you can greatly assist the mechanic's inspection of the transmission. You have already seriously driven the car over various road conditions, and can tell him if anything seems out of kilter. Shaking, shimmying, poor acceleration, occasional dying of the engine, or rough shifting can be due to many different things besides transmission problems. But telling the mechanic about any problem you're worried about (aside from personal ones) will get him on the track of discovering any problem the car may have.

4. The Cooling System.

As previously discussed in chapter three, the cooling system is a an extremely crucial system for the running of your car. Basically, your car is powered by a series of explosions. The car's cooling system is what controls these explosions—the same way that the cooling system in a nuclear power plant controls its fission reaction. If the car's cooling system is not working correctly, your engine will eventually "melt down". While it won't give off a radioactive cloud, it will still leave you feeling just as sick. You want your mechanic to check this system out very closely. Have him check the system over for leaks and corrosion. Pressure testing the cooling system is a very simple task—it only takes a few minutes and can be accomplished while your mechanic is performing other checks. Once the pressure tester has been pumped up, it can just be left on for five minutes as the mechanic goes about checking other things. It is definitely not a test you should pay extra for.

If you have any worries about the car's cooling system (or if you wish to be extremely conservative), you can have your mechanic perform a carbon monoxide leak test on the cooling system. Carbon monoxide is an exhaust gas produced by the explosions occurring inside the engine. It should only appear in the car's exhaust system. If your mechanic discovers carbon monoxide existing inside the cooling system, there is a leak somewhere inside the engine. Normally such a car has other symptoms that would alert a good mechanic. He would tell you his suspicions and ask if you wanted him to perform the test. It should only cost you twenty dollars or so. Taking into consideration the extremely high cost of repairing internal engine problems, this small fee is something you should consider.

Your mechanic should check the cooling fan system of your car. If it has a mechanical belt driven radiator fan, the fan clutch should be checked for proper operation. If it has an electric radiator cooling fan(s), it should be checked for proper cycling operation. And if it has air conditioning, the auxiliary cooling fan should be checked for operation—especially if you live in a hot climate like Texas. These checks would only take a few minutes. As the car will be running during much of the mechanic's checks anyway, the cooling fan(s) will be operating and are easily watched while other checks are being made. You might ask your mechanic about cooling fan operation if you suspect the temperature gauge was running too high during your own road test. And if your chosen car does not have a temperature gauge in it, you should definitely ask him to check the cooling fan operation out closely.

5. The Car's Charging System.

Your mechanic should check the car's charging system for proper operation. It only takes him a few minutes to hook his diagnosis equipment to the charging system. He can quickly discover if the alternator is putting out the correct voltage and amperage. The battery itself can be checked to a certain degree, although even professional mechanics have questioned the validity of various battery testing equipment. (I could include five page technical articles here, but trust me on this one. Battery testing equipment is generally unreliable, and in some cases the test itself can damage a battery.) Luckily, batteries are a cheap item in today's competitive economy, and they are easily replaced. If the battery in a used car looks old to me, I usually advise my customers to put a new one in if they purchase the car. The hassle of being stranded out in the boondocks by a dead battery just isn't worth $42.95.

While checking out the car's charging system, your mechanic can give you an overall picture of the car's electrical wiring system. He can tell you if the wiring is in good condition, or whether wires are frayed and melted. He can also tell you if the wiring harness is in its original factory condition, or if it has been repaired numerous times in patchwork fashion. If you have noticed any strange or malfunctioning electrical part of the car, be sure to tell your mechanic. Even something as minor as a flickering bulb, or a radio that is acting strange can be important to tell him. They may be symptoms of a deeper electrical problem lurking in the car.

The entire metal body of the car is charged with negative twelve volt electricity—it serves as the ground system for the car's electrics. The complete electrical system of your car is interconnected through this grounding system. If there is an electrical grounding problem in a car, it can create some very weird symptoms through these grounding connections. Headlights may surprisingly turn themselves on when you step on the brake pedal. The horn may decide to beep when you put on the turn signals. So if you notice anything electrical in the car that does not seem to be functioning correctly, be sure to let your mechanic know. It will help him discover if the problem is serious, or if it's just something small like a bulb beginning to burn out its filament.

6. The Car's Braking System.

Your mechanic should inspect the vehicle's braking system, including the emergency brakes. Tell him anything odd you have noticed about the brakes, including the following:

A. Whether they're pulling to one side, indicating uneven braking power.

B. If they're making strange noises when applied, indicating possible worn out linings. As previously discussed, many later model cars now have non- asbestos brake linings which can make odd noises at times. Your mechanic can physically inspect the linings during his check out. He can explain if the noises are normal for your car, or if the linings are actually worn out.

C. If the pedal is falling to the floor when pushed hard, indicating a leak somewhere in the system.

D. If the steering wheel begins to shimmy when the brakes are applied harshly, indicating possible warpage in the front brake system.

E. If the emergency braking system is functioning with enough power to hold the car stationary on inclines.

F. If any brake system warning lights have come on during your road test. This includes both warning lights that remain on constantly, and lights which momentarily come on.

Any mechanic can certainly discover these braking aspects himself, but your added information will greatly facilitate the process. Besides, when talking to the mechanic, you might discover details about braking systems that will serve yourself twofold:

First, you can have peace of mind understanding what is right and wrong with your car's brakes. Brakes are the most important safety item in any car. They change the tremendous kinetic energy of a speeding car into heat; transforming a potentially deadly flying object into a completely safe motionless one. I realize that we all take cars for granted in our modern hustle bustle society. This can be a good thing considering all the other maddening issues society throws at us on a daily basis. But you should never take your brakes completely for granted. A little knowledge and occasional physical checks of the brakes can give you true peace of mind.

Second, you can protect yourself from being "ripped off" by dishonest brake repairmen who may not be as truthful as your check out mechanic. All brake systems wear out (unless you happen to live in some previously undiscovered frictionless environment). If you own a car any moderate length of time, you will eventually need to have the brakes fixed. It's to your advantage to learn a little about your car's braking system. As previously discussed in chapter three, asbestos has been banned from use in car's brake linings. The newer materials used often have the negative side effect of being rather noisy. Just because you hear noises when the brakes are applied, do not think you need a brake job. In a car that is new to you, this noise is telling you to have the brake linings physically checked out for wear. But if your mechanic tells you they are fine, and the noise is just normal for this particular car, you have learned something very useful. A little knowledge can keep the wrong hands out of your pockets.

Brake repairs are not normally very expensive repairs with most car models, unless the entire system has been damaged in a flood or the car itself is ancient history (being more than twenty years old). But if your car has ABS (anti lock braking system), make sure your mechanic checks the brakes out with a fine tooth comb. ABS systems do create a much safer vehicle in slippery situations, but they have come at a price (and not just that extra price you pay for the car). ABS systems have taken a relatively simple hydraulic brake system and have turned it into a computer driven hydraulic/electronic network. Repairs are often complex and VERY expensive, so be sure to have your mechanic take a good look.

7. The Car's Frame And Body.

You'll want your mechanic to check out all possible frame or body damage. If you've noticed anything suspect about the car's body, be sure to tell him. This would included wrinkled body panels, misaligned body parts with uneven gaps, freshly painted areas, non-matching paint color, and the discovery of paint overspray anywhere on the car. Your mechanic can decide if the car has been in a serious wreck, if it's just been in a fender-bender, or if the car is a "cream puff" and has never been hit. There are many cars out there that have been in medium sized accidents. They are still dependable modes of transportation when they have been professionally repaired. Their resale value is certainly lower than a non-wrecked car, but this can be to your advantage. Assuming the car has been correctly repaired (your check out mechanic can discover this), you can save hundreds or even thousands of dollars by purchasing a previously damaged vehicle. I have personally owned three cars that had been in medium-sized wrecks, and all three served me faithfully for many years.

Checking out a car for possible wreck damage is where your mechanic's years of experience really come into play. His expansive knowledge and discerning eye knows what is normal in a car's body and what isn't. All cars have many welded seams in them, especially with modern day unibody cars that lack a true separate frame. Your mechanic can discover if these welds are the original factory made welds, or if they are the result of later accident related body repair work. As an example, I was checking out a small pick up truck for Fred on a hot summer day. He had been using the air conditioner at full blast, and had noticed whistling noises coming from the driver's door area when he was driving at highway speeds. I looked at the door and noticed it was misaligned. The gap between the body of the truck and the door was much larger in the front of the door than it was at the back of the door. After opening the hood, I discovered some very poorly finished welds. These welds went around the entire width of the truck—they were used to connect the front of the truck to the back. This is not how trucks are built, so I checked the serial number of the truck's engine with the serial number of its body. The numbers did not match at all, and after calling the dealership with these registration numbers, I discovered the truth. The front of the truck was from a 1986 truck, but the remainder of the truck was a 1989 truck. This was a two-for-one sale that no one would want to participate in (other than the dishonest seller).

So be sure to inform your mechanic about anything that has made you feel "a little odd" about the car's body. No matter how small you may think it is, like a tail light lens that is slightly out of alignment, because it may be hiding something bigger underneath. Then let your mechanic survey the structural soundness of the car. A few minutes with a well-trained eye will catch any important flaws.

8. Whether The Car Has Been Flooded Out.

You want your mechanic to discover if the car has been flooded out. As previously discussed, floodwater can do severe damage to modern day computer controlled vehicles. You want your mechanic to check for any possible signs that the car has been flooded out. Have him look for any signs of mildewy odors under the seats or inside the trunk. Any evidence of heavy rusting inside the car's passenger area points towards a car's being in a flood. The same hold true for massive stains in the car's interior—if they all end at the same level, the car has been flooded out. If you have any suspicions about the car being in a flood, be sure to tell your mechanic. He can then check the car out very deliberately, looking in every nook and cranny for possible flooding evidence.

9. The Car's Suspension And Steering Systems.

The last major aspects that everyone should have their mechanic check are the car's suspension and steering systems. In the old golden days of cardom (that have long since passed us by), checking the suspension system was a relatively simple process. All cars had simple shock absorber systems. Pushing down on the car at each corner, and watching how the car bounced back was a perfectly good test of the suspension system. If the car rebounded smoothly with only a small amount of bouncing, the shocks were in good shape. But if the car continued to bounce up and down like a car in an old black and white cartoon, the shocks were completely worn out. Today's more complex vehicles usually have MacPherson struts instead of plain shock absorbers, and such a test would not be a very useful one.

Modern cars often contain a very complex system of torsion bars with each wheel having its own completely independent suspension system. You need an expert mechanic to inspect these systems for possible problems. Any good mechanic can inspect the steering and suspension systems for leakage and worn-out parts, and you can assist him immensely. Tell him anything that does not "feel right" about the car's handling:

1. Whether the car pulls to one side when driving on a level surface.

2. Whether the steering wheel shakes at any speeds, even if this shaking goes away at a higher or a lower speed.

3. Whether the car corners correctly, or if it either understeers or oversteers. (Understeering is when a car does not follow your turning of the steering wheel—it takes too many turns of the steering wheel for the car to properly turn a corner. Oversteering is the exact opposite—the car turns a corner too tightly with a small movement of the steering wheel.)

4. Whether the car handles bumps and holes in the road relatively smoothly, or if it bounces and you feel a loss of control during bumpy driving. This loss of control should be checked for both at city and highway driving speeds.

Giving this information to your mechanic will greatly facilitate his task, and may also help you understand how your particular model should operate. A long wheel based luxury car is going to ride smoother than a short wheel based sports car, regardless of the suspension tricks that are built into the sports car. As an example, I recently checked out a beautiful red sports car for Emily. I gave the car a thorough examination, and it passed with flying colors. But I did tell Emily that the suspension system in this particular car was a special racing type set-up. I mentioned that she should expect a relatively rough ride, especially in bumpy city driving. This car was designed for good high speed cornering—not for smooth effortless city cruising. Emily was glad to hear this, as she had forgotten to ask me if the car's suspension system had any problems (she thought it might have been riding too rough). Discovering that this relatively rough ride was normal for her particular model, she was happy with the car and bought it that same day.

Your mechanic should check your car's suspension and steering systems for leaks and cracked seals, especially around the power steering system (if so equipped). Power steering systems operate at extremely high pressures. They will often be the first system to leak in any car with more than fifty thousand miles on the odometer. Power steering system repairs can run from fifty dollars to replace a hose, to five hundred dollars (or more) if the steering rack itself is leaking. But any repair cost would be deducted from the car's selling price. Your mechanic can search for any of these problems, and give you the cost to deduct from the car's worth. And if he discovers a problem in the suspension/steering systems while road testing the car, but is not able to discover its underlying cause, he can send you to a front end specialist if the problem seems excessive. I've had a handful of customers who ended up purchasing used cars in this manner. Their front ends (or I should say their car's front ends) had shaking problems whose underlying causes were not obvious to me. I could have given an educated guess, but instead I sent them down the street to a very good front end specialist. He gave them all written estimates on the repair cost of their problems. They were all happy and purchased their cars, deducting the repair cost from the cars' values.

THINGS YOU MAY WANT YOUR MECHANIC TO CHECK

The following section includes additional aspects of your car that you may want your mechanic to check out. This section incorporates options that some cars have and some cars don't have. It may also include aspects of your car that you just don't care about—such as electrically heated seats or sun roofs that you never plan on opening. So just skip the sections that don't interest you.

1. The Car's Air Conditioning System.

With laws concerning freon changing almost daily, air conditioning work is becoming more complicated (and much more expensive). Mechanics have to purchase very expensive recycling equipment, and need various certifications for working on air conditioning systems. As usual, the consumer (you) ends up bearing the brunt of this added expense. So if you plan on using your car's air conditioner frequently, you should have your mechanic check it out closely. Now is the time to have the system checked out, don't wait until later to discover the possibility of expensive repairs lurking inside all that cold air. A quick electronic leak detector test can be run on the system, especially if you have any worries about the system not cooling down correctly. But even a car that's cooling down today may not be tomorrow—thanks to the oldest trick in the air conditioning book. The used car with a leaking AC system is simply filled up with freon before you come to check the car out. As air conditioning freon leaks can take anywhere from five minutes to five years before the system is empty, this refilling may fool you. The AC may feel cold enough, but in such a car the freon is leaking out bit by bit. You can't see it, because freon is an invisible gas. But no leak can hide from a good mechanic equipped with a state of the art leak detector. Today's electronic leak detectors are extremely sensitive, and can discover even a small leak that would take years to stop the AC from blowing cold. You may have to pay a small extra fee to have the system leak-checked, but considering the high cost of most AC repairs, this is money well spent. Especially if you have any suspicions that the ac is not acting "just right".

2. The Car's Tires.

You may want your mechanic to give you a report on the tires. Have him discover if they are all the same size and brand tire, or whether they're a combination of different brands or sizes. Even though cars have the same size rims for all four tires, it is possible to fit a variety of different size tires on these same rims. You should be sure that all the tires are the same exact size. And while you're at it, ask your mechanic about the brand of tires that the car has on it. By law, all tires have to include their country of origin to be printed on the sidewall of the tire itself. I have personally seen some extremely cheap tires manufactured in Taiwan that did not last even four thousand miles. Both car lots and private individuals have been known to purchase the absolute cheapest tires for a car they're selling because the old tires were completely shot. They may look nice and shiny now, with plenty of tread, but they won't last very long. AND IF YOU EVENTUALLY PURCHASE THE CAR, BE SURE TO EXAMINE THE TIRES AGAIN BEFORE MONEY CHANGES HANDS. A very old seller's trick is to swap the car's tires for cheaper brands or completely worn out ones. To ensure that this doesn't happen to you, have your mechanic write down the size and brands of tires that are on the car now.

3. The Car's Power Windows And Power Sun Roof.

The cost of repairing power windows and sun roofs has drastically increased over the past few years. This is due to the use of many unitized parts (which have to be replaced as a unit and can not be repaired separately) and because standardization is severely lacking within these systems. Different manufacturers often use completely unrelated systems, so little or no aftermarket parts are available when repairs are needed. (Translation—you have to go to the dealer to buy these parts. If anything relatively big is wrong with the system, the parts will be expensive. Monopolization is not a joyful thing, unless you happen to be the one owning the monopoly.) Even within a particular car model, it is commonplace for each window to use a separate motor that is not interchangeable with any other window's motor. You should have checked the operation of these devices during your own inspection of the car, but it only takes your mechanic a couple minutes to check them out further. He can tell you if their operation is smooth, and if there are any unusual noises coming from them. Even if you are not very interested in whether the back windows work or whether the sun roof opens, have him inspect them. You can deduct their repair cost from the car's purchase price, even if you have no intention of ever repairing them.

4. The Operation Of The Car's Seats (Electrical or Manual).

You may think the operation of the car's seats isn't that big of a deal. But just try driving a car on a three hour trip with a seat that's too close or too far away from the pedals. And if a seat is broken, this may be merely a symptom of a deeper problem. I've seen many cars with non-functioning or poorly operating seat adjusters. A few of them didn't work because the car had been in a wreck and the car's frame was out of alignment. And some of them had been flooded out, causing the seat bottoms to rust and become very stubborn about changing their position. As you can well imagine, electrically adjustable seats are even more susceptible to water damage, so their operation should be checked closely.

Be sure to check all the adjustable seats in the car, don't stop once the driver's seat has been inspected. All cars have adjustable passenger seats, and some luxury cars have independent adjusters for every seat in the car. It only takes a minute to check their operation; an infinitesimal fragment of time compared to the hundreds of hours your posterior (and your friends') will be resting on them. And while you're at it, pull off the seat covers if your car has any. Find out if the seats underneath them look like something the cat dragged in, or if they are in reasonably good shape. Reupholstering seats is not cheap, and replacing physically broken seats with new ones is even more expensive. There is absolutely nothing wrong with using a good set of seat covers for cosmetics and for physical comfort—but you should pay less for a car that has worn out seats lying under them.

5. The Car's Entertainment System.

In the olden days, your car may have had an am radio, or if you were really lucky, an am/fm radio. Today's cars have radios, cassette players, and even multi-disc cd players. Checking their basic operation can be done by you—see if the radio works, if the cassettes play, or if the cds function correctly.(Checking more complex systems, such as multi-function cd players, may require an in-depth manual and a computer whiz to entirely grasp the beast's inner workings, if you care to go that far.) In cars that have a factory installed entertainment system, this is all you need to know—that the system is playing music correctly. But if your car's system is an aftermarket one which was installed by a car stereo store, or by (gasp!) its owner, you may want your mechanic to look at its wiring system. The entertainment system may have not been compatibly wired into your car's electrical system. This incorrect wiring may eventually cause problems, as the following illustrates graphically. Gerome had a very expensive Italian sports car, and an inkling for extremely loud classical music. He decided to go to a local automotive specialty shop to purchase a fifteen hundred dollar multi-disc cd system. The store obliged him, and installed the system in his car that afternoon. But they had not wired the system compatibly with the car's electrics, and smoke began coming out of his dash on the drive home. To make a long story short, the music store's insurance company had to shell out five thousand dollars to repair the sports car's electrical system. Granted, this is an extreme example, but I have seen incorrectly wired stereo systems cause alternators and other expensive electrical components of a car to burn out. If you don't know whether your car has a factory system or an aftermarket one, mention it to your mechanic and he can advise you if any further checking is necessary.

6. The Car's Mileage Reading On Its Odometer.

The last extra thing you may want to ask your mechanic to check concerns the odometer's mileage reading. Ask him if it seems to be an accurate figure, in his professional opinion. As previously discussed, there are laws concerning setting back speedometers or changing them out with new or used units that have lower mileage readings on them. If you are purchasing the car from a professional sales person, be sure to have them show you a copy of the mileage certificate. If you are purchasing the car from a private individual, ask to see some repair or maintenance receipts that have the car's mileage written on them. Make sure the figures are in a logical sequence that matches the mileage presently on the odometer. Then have your mechanic do a little detective work:

First, have him check if the odometer is working when he road tests the car. Many car odometers are driven by plastic gears which can do very strange things as they wear out. They can give wildly inaccurate readings, both high and low, or they may only function sporadically. And if your chosen car has a computer digitalized speedometer, virtually anything can occur when the electronics malfunction. I have seen digital speedometers read one hundred miles per hour when the car was obviously going about ten mph.

Second, have him look over any repair or maintenance receipts that you have managed to procure from the seller. He may be able to better assess the truthfulness of these receipts, by comparing them with the actual repairs that have been done on the car. As you can imagine, it is not very hard to create false receipts for the purpose of validating an odometer that has been set back (it's a big world out there and sometimes it can get very nasty). If your mechanic discovers that much of the work included in these receipts has never been actually done on the vehicle, be very leery about the mileage figures they contain.

Third, have your mechanic play Sherlock Holmes and attempt to discover any mileage information that may lurk in the nooks and crannies of the car. Old forgotten oil change stickers, old inspections stickers, and old repair receipts all contain mileage figures on them. I have personally discovered quite a few of them inside glove boxes, on the bottom of trunks, fallen between or under seats, and even hiding on various door jambs of cars. Most times they validate the actual mileage on the odometer, but in a few cases they showed a car that had much higher mileage on it.

Fourth, if your mechanic feels in his professional opinion that the mileage figure on the car is accurate, ask him if he can take a guess at what type of mileage this has been. Tell him you understand this is just an educated guess on his behalf (unless he has known the previous owner), but that you are curious about his opinion. Intensive bumper to bumper city driving will wear a car out four to five times faster than a heavy diet of highway driving. All those advertisements you see about cars lasting one hundred, two hundred, or three hundred thousand miles are based on this fact. These long distance vehicles have spent a great deal of their lives driving on highways. Their wear and tear has been greatly reduced when compared to equivalent city mileage, and they can still be in excellent condition. As an example, clutches often wear out in standard transmission cars after sixty thousand miles. But I have seen basically highway driven cars that still had the original clutch in them after two hundred thousand miles. Your mechanic is not a magic genie, but he can give you an idea if your car has been mainly subjected to these easy highway miles, or if it has led a harsher city life.

THE FINAL WRAP-UP

When your mechanic has finished checking out your car, have a little discussion with him. Ask him how he rates the car—whether it's in mint condition, whether it's one step away from the junk yard, or whether it's somewhere in between. (Most cars are like most people, landing in that somewhere in between category.) If he feels the car is a very bad deal, take his advice and look at another car—there are literally thousands of them out there! The small check out fee that you pay him is not wasted money, it is money well spent. It's kept you from shoveling your hard earned cash into a bottomless money-pit car. If he gives the car a thumbs up, be happy, but don't end your discussion there. Have him give you a list of every single thing he has found wrong with the car. No matter how small or petty. And get repair cost estimates for all these problems, especially for any relatively expensive repairs—even if you have absolutely no interest in repairing them. You may not care one hoot about that six inch dent in the rear fender, but it lowers the value of the car by hundreds of dollars. You want to have every bit of leverage during the bargaining process. Use all the information your mechanic has discovered to tip the scales towards your side.

Lastly, have your mechanic give you his professional opinion on the car's actual value. Of course, this is a highly subjective opinion, as car values often fluctuate as quickly as the weather changes. But any mechanic worth his salt can give you a good ball-park figure. He can tell you if your chosen model is presently a very hot number, and that you won't be able to barter much on the price. Four wheel drive sport utility vehicles and convertibles are always very hot items. As are small estate-sized station wagons during the spring and summer months, when families go vacationing. You can expect to pay more for these hot items, but remember—you are buying a used car and will save money regardless. Just take a gander at the sticker prices on brand new models if you want to be reassured. And if your chosen car isn't winning today's popularity contest, so much the better. You can barter to your heart's content—which brings us to the next chapter.

Chapter 5

CUTTING THE DEAL – HORSETRADING SECRETS

Now it's time to cut the deal—to decide on the purchase price of your chosen vehicle. This is one of the few remaining areas in our modern society where you can still do some serious bartering over an item's actual price. Buying a used car is not like shopping at the local mega-mart where the prices are all set down in black-and-white. You'll get some pretty strange looks from the cashier if you attempt to haggle over the price of a shirt in any of these stores. Buying a used car is a bartering process with all the bells and whistles (or as we say in Texas, a real dog and pony show). All sorts of games are played during this process, both on the buying and the selling ends. You're much better off with some knowledge of the unwritten rules and the many "tricks" that are played once the game has begun.

The first and foremost part of the game is discovering how much money you are going to pay for the car. Commonly, the seller's asking price will be ridiculously high. To counter this, the potential buyer's offer will be ridiculously low to compensate for this overinflated asking price. The actual selling price that the car goes for is based on many different interrelated variables, but they can be broken down into the following:

1. How Are You Going To Pay For The Car?

This is often the most crucial part of the car's eventual sales price. If you are paying cash, you are in the best of all positions and have a strong bartering tool on your side. (For all intents and purposes, money obtained from financing the car outside of the person actually selling the car is treated the same as cash. The seller will still be receiving a lump sum of cash when the deal is over.) If you have to finance the car through the seller, you are in a very poor bartering position. The seller has you at his advantage—he is fronting you the money and can practically name his own price. You may decide upon financing the car through the seller, after carefully comparing the interest rates and down payment requirements—although it is extremely rare to receive the best deal through any seller. But if you have to finance the car through its seller because it's the only option you have, you are not going to cut a very good price. You may get the seller to come down a little from the asking price, but this is usually a very hollow victory. The asking price is known in the business as the "sucker" price, an overinflated figure that only a completely unknowledgeable person would pay. You need to "beg, borrow, or steal" money from any source that you possibly can, in order to make your bartering position a strong one.

As an example, Sherry had found a nice two door sports/sedan sitting on a used car lot. The asking price was ninety-five hundred dollars. But she had done some researching on the car's actual value, and knew this asking price was absurd. After only twenty minutes of bartering, she had gotten the lot to lower the price to sixty-five hundred dollars. This was mainly due to the fact that she was paying cash for the car—cash she was borrowing from her credit union. Not only was she getting a good price on the car, but her credit union also gave her free life insurance to cover the loan—something which she would have paid a premium for at the lot. If you absolutely just can't get financing anywhere else but from the seller, I will give you some tips to make the best of a bad situation later in this chapter. But try as hard as you can to get money elsewhere—it's worth even a Herculean effort to achieve this great bartering tool.

2. What Is The Car's Base Worth?

The question of a car's actual worth is certainly a rather subjective one. As previously discussed, it's dependent upon many variables—the age of the car, the mechanical shape the car is in, the pristineness of the car's paint and bodywork, the mileage the car has, whether it's a one-owner car, and whether it's presently a hot model that people are climbing over each other to buy. All these variables working together allow the actual value of the car to fluctuate quite a bit. But you can assess a base value to any car. There are many car value books out there—the blue books, the red books, and so on. They give value fluctuations for individual car models; basing their values on such factors as high mileage/low mileage, average or immaculate condition, two door or four door, and so on. The books can often be too high in some of their values, but the loan value of the car included in these books is a good base value for assessing what your car is actually worth. You will probably pay more than the loan value for the car (if the car is in excellent shape), but it's a very good figure to use as a working base.

An even better way to get a good idea on the car's base value (aside from the figure given to you by your mechanic) is to simply call up your insurance agent. Tell your agent that you are thinking about purchasing a used car. Give him (or her) the year model, how many miles are on it, what general shape the car's paint and bodywork is in, and then sit back while the insurance computer runs. Then just ask your agent for a ballpark figure on how much money you would receive if the car was totalled in a wreck or was stolen. But BE SURE to tell him/her that you want this information because that is what you believe is the true value that you wish to pay for the car. Reassure your agent that you are not planning some insurance scam; you just want to take precautions against paying too much for a car, and then losing this extra money if the car was totalled. They will gladly give you the information. And if you're looking for financing help, you might even get a two-for-one-here. Many insurance companies are now financing cars at a competitive rate, so you should enquire about financing if you are thinking about going that route.

3. What Have You (And Your Mechanic) Found Wrong With The Car?

The imperfections that have been discovered in your chosen vehicle are the best bartering tools you have. A lack of imperfections can raise the base value of the car some—but nothing lowers the base value of a car faster than the discovery of problems (even if they mean nothing to you). Absolutely every single thing that you've found to be askew in the car should be written down and used for ammunition—no matter how small it seems. Cracked windshields, small dents, fading paint, small oil leaks, and even non-functioning windshield squirters should be used to lower the car's price. Larger problems, complete with your mechanic's estimates on their repair cost, are an obvious way to lower the car's value—but small ones can often be just as important. They help set-up the overall tone of the bartering process, showing the seller that you are going to be in control of the situation—not the other way around. Knowledge may indeed be a dangerous thing, but in this case it's not dangerous to you—it's dangerous to the seller.

4. Who Is Selling The Car?

The question of who is selling the car may not seem like a very important one at first glance, but it can greatly affect the eventual sales price. Regardless of who is selling the car, be it a professional sales person or an individual owner, you need to do a little personality detective work. A professional sales person is selling cars for a living— it's a strictly business deal to them. The car definitely has no sentimental value to a sales person. On the other hand, an individual selling their own car may have some "feelings" towards the car that tend to raise their own image of the car's value. You have to gain some understanding of the personality behind the sale, in order to further your own intentions (of paying the lowest possible price). For clarification, this will be broken down into two sections: A. The private individual selling their own car. And B. The professional sales person.

A. Dealing with a private individual selling their own car is the route many people feel to be the best. It is often a very good way to purchase a car—IF you are a good barterer and a decent reader of people and their personalties. If the individual seller seems to have an emotional feel for the car, you can even use this to your own advantage. Tell him/her that you will take very good care of the car—you plan on garaging it whenever possible, you'll change the oil every three thousand miles, you'll wax the car every month, and so on. But say this matter-of-factly, don't EVER get too openly excited about any car, because this will tilt the bartering process in favor of the seller. Be courteous with an individual selling their own car, but don't attempt to become "best buddies" with them (unless, of course, you happen to be buying the car from a friend—and everyone has heard the old saying, "never buy a car from a friend—you will gain a car but will lose a friend.")

Even if a private individual doesn't show obvious emotional feelings towards the car, he/she will have monetary feelings. Unfortunately for you, these feelings can often cause the seller's asking price to be up there in the stratosphere. If you find yourself dealing with such a person, you need to bring them down from the clouds and back to Earth. As a general fact, people tend to greatly overestimate the actual value of just about anything they own. As an example, take your diamond ring for an appraisal at the local jewelry shop. Then ask the jeweler what he would pay you cash for that same diamond ring. If you do get an actual price, it will certainly bring you back down to Earth about the diamond's cash value. When purchasing a used car, you get to use this evaluation process in your favor (for once!). Explain to the seller that money is tight today, and you are paying cash (the only way to deal with an individual owner). Tell him/her that you are taking a gamble, as there are no guarantees when buying a car from a private individual. This gambling with your hard earned cash should be reflected in the car's true value, which is why you are going to pay less for the car. Certainly the guarantees which used car lots often give aren't worth the paper they're printed on (as they can be full of loopholes and restrictions). But you don't need to mention this to your individual seller. Remember, bartering is a game—you and your mechanic have already decided that the car is a good one to buy. Now you have to play the game of highball/lowball—and good games playing here may save you hundreds of dollars. I've even seen great bartering game players save thousands of dollars by taking a very firm stance on what they're going to pay and not budging up at all.

With an individual seller, attempting to discover how badly he/she needs to sell their car is perhaps the most crucial aspect of bringing the car's price down. To get the best price possible, you want to find out just how much time the seller has to play with. Does the seller have a deadline closing in where he/she absolutely has to have the car sold? Or can he/she wait until Hades freezes over before a high purchase price is achieved? Try your people reading skills on this, in conjunction with your common sense—as the following illustrates. Paul had just returned to the United States after a few years spent "down under" in the land of kangaroos. He was driving a clunker that a friend sold him cheap, but he wanted a classy set of wheels for weekend use. After spying an advertisement in the local paper for a classic 1966 American "dinosaurmobile", he drove over to the seller's house for a look. After a short discussion, Paul discovered that the seller was in a real bind for some hard cold cash. He needed four thousand dollars by Sunday, and was going to sell any of his four vehicles to procure the money. Paul, being a good gambler, decided to come back on Sunday with some cash. No one had purchased the Fordasaurus, so he bought it for thirty five hundred dollars—even though the car had been appraised by an independent assessor of classic cars for eighty-five hundred. When Paul brought me the car for servicing, I was truly amazed by the showroom mint condition the car was in, considering its twenty-eight year old age. A little people reading combined with some look-around common sense can go a long way. Especially if you're dealing with a private individual selling a car.

B. Dealing with a professional sales person contains similar bartering gambits (from here on I will use the word salesman, for brevity and reasons already discussed in Chapter 2). Only here the ante has been raised. You are now dealing with a person who makes their living selling used cars. No matter how strong he comes on to you as a game show host ready to hand over the car keys for practically nothing, do not be fooled. This is not a game show, this is a bartering war. You must remember at all times that HE IS NOT GOING TO EVER GIVE YOU ANYTHING FOR FREE. You will have to fight for every inch of ground—for a lower purchase price, for a lower interest rate (if you finance through the lot), and for a higher trade-in price (if you are trading your old car). You must disregard any freebies that may have been advertised with the purchase of any car—whether they are free television sets, free rust-proofing, or even free gasoline for a year. These offers are not free, they are merely added to the price you pay for the car, and they are reflected in the car's sales price and the interest rate you pay for financing. Likewise, be extremely wary of any guarantees—such as a thirty day satisfaction guarantee on any car you buy. Most satisfaction guarantees only serve to satisfy the lot's bank account. If you aren't satisfied by the car, they will let you return the car, but they won't return your money. They will merely allow to you apply your money towards another car that's on the lot (and often will not let you barter much over the next car's price).

When dealing with a professional salesman, always remember, YOU MUST CONTROL THE SITUATION. I have listened to many sales technique tapes that were in the cassette decks of my own customer's cars. These customers were all salespeople, and used the tapes to brush up their selling techniques while they were driving from appointment to appointment. Every single tape urged the salespeople to always control the selling situation, and to NEVER allow the customer to take over this control. If you really want to hone up your bartering skills for a one-on-one session with a professional salesmen, you might consider listening to one of these sales technique tapes. Many libraries carry them, or a book version, so it wouldn't cost you anything. If you do decide to check one out, just take in all the information and apply it in reverse. Any of you who feel overwhelmed by salesmen and very uncomfortable with their games should try this. You'll be surprised to discover the very basic methods that underlie salesmen's attempts to wrestle that cold hard cash out of your hands. Armed with a greater knowledge of their plan of attack, you can have your own counter-attack prepared. Certainly there is a great deal of free-wheeling that occurs during the bartering process, but you will fare much better if you have a good grasp of the basic game plan.

Your own basic game plan with any professional salesman should be extremely simple. You have the ultimate control, because you are the one spending the money. (This is also why you should never finance a car through a lot, because then they have the money and are loaning it to you. You have lost most of your control over the bartering process.) You can walk away at any moment, leaving the salesman high and dry. And believe me, the salesmen are acutely aware of this fact, however much they may attempt to hide it. Salesmen know that over ninety percent of those leaving their lot without purchasing a car will never purchase a car from them. They have a name for these people—they call them "come-backers". Salesmen live in fear of having endless weeks where nobody but non-buying come-backers show up on their lots.

Practically every single used car salesman in the world is working on straight commission. With no sales, they make no money. About the only thing they are provided with by the car lot owner is a desk and a telephone. This "living on the edge" often make salesmen a strange breed to deal with, but you can turn this to your own advantage. Used car salesmen are deathly afraid that you are going to walk away from their lot, and buy somewhere else. Your ability to freely walk away is your ace in the hole. As long as you continue to control the bartering process and don't allow the salesman to usurp this control, you are truly in the driver's seat. You don't want to overuse your ace to take control, continually threatening to leave the lot,because then the salesman might decide that you are a waste of time for him. He might give you a cursory sales try and then look for an easier customer. Show the salesman that you are not going to be bullied around by heavy handed sales tactics by being calm and knowledgeable about the bartering process. Tell him you're seriously looking for a car, and that this seriousness includes comparing cars and prices that other used car lots have. (Of course you have already done this comparing before you begin seriously bartering over a particular car's price. But you don't need to let the salesman know this.) This more subtle threat that you are going to walk off the lot often works wonders. The salesman, who is already worrying that you may walk off the lot never to return again, is now worried that the price he's giving you is not competitive with others you may procure. Your controlling the bartering process should force him to give you a much better price than was originally asked. You should expect to put in a little time here (perhaps as long as half an hour), because the salesman will often play games, such as "I have to get my boss to ok this offer". This is often a complete lie, just to stall you and make the process last longer. The salesman will always try to make your price lowering attempts long and arduous. He sees this cutting into his profit—the lower the sales price, the lower his commission. And the one thing salesmen do have is time. You have to realize that some time will be wasted on his behalf, it's just the nature of the game. But you can't let this time be excessive.

The thirty minute period already mentioned serves as a good base. If the salesman starts wasting more time than this, you can suggest that it's time for a stroll to some other lot. You may even physically begin to walk away. Any serious salesman would rather make a hundred dollars than none at all. Admittedly the process of bartering with a used car salesman can be like pulling teeth at times, but always remember—you're the one who should be playing the dentist. Continue to wrestle control of the situation away from the salesman, and don't let any of his sales gimmicks take you off track. Practically everything the salesman will say is a gimmick used to hide the fact that he's attempting to squeeze every penny he can out of you. Used car salesman have one solitary purpose in life—to procure as much money for used cars as possible. And it doesn't matter how this money is paid—whether it's "front end" money of a large purchase price and/or large down payment; or "back end" money of a high interest rate. You are the one who will be paying this money out, so don't be fooled by the salesman rearranging the furniture. All this rearranging through salesman gimmicks can lead to an almost infinite level of complexity—something you want to avoid at all costs. You control the situation by bartering strictly over three possible factors—1. the car's price, 2. the car's downpayment, and 3. the financing interest rate and length of loan. When paying cash, this process is further simplified by dealing only with factor one, the car's selling price.

Cash is indeed King in the used car world, and for a knowledgeable buyer it will always reign supreme. Cash allows you to barter from the strongest position—you have the money and the salesmen want to get their commission percentage of it. Think of them as a pack of hungry dogs who haven't eaten lately. You have the food in your hands and decide who is going to be fed, and how much you are going to feed them. Don't let any salesman become a wolf and frighten or confuse you with their tactics—keep them tame and on-guard with all the previous knowledge you've gained. Don't let them smell blood and close in for the kill with wild sales tactics. If you feel your particular salesman is not going to deal the way you want, ask the manager for another one. But don't let your salesman himself send you to another salesman on the lot, because this is an old sales gambit commonly used on lots. The salesmen on the lot will often attempt to wear you down with a pack mentality, just like wolves hunting a strong prey. If they see you as a tough sell, they will often hand you over to a fresh salesman friend. Do not accept this treatment, because it will be playing right into their hands. You need to control the situation, so it is you who chooses a different salesman. NEVER allow your first salesman to "bring in a friend" to help you. Choose your own salesperson, and turn the tables on them.

Here you may well ask, how do I go about choosing the right salesman for me? Much of this choice depends on your own self-knowledge. If you feel bartering is something you're very good at, you may want to choose the salesman who has all those "salesman of the month" awards hanging on his wall. Such a salesman does sell a great deal of cars, and if you feel ready to go head to head with a pro, you might cut a good deal. A salesman who pushes many cars out the door has a great deal of pull at the lot, and this power can allow him to cut a lower price on the car. Because once you have gotten the price of a used car down close to the absolute lowest figure that the lot will sell it for, this low offer will have to be approved by the lot manager/owner. Admittedly, you'll have to do some good bartering and spend a deal of your own time to reach this level. But if you can do it, a high volume salesman can best finish off this deal. He can explain to the manager that you are a tough customer, and the manager will know that it's true, since his best salesman is telling him so. In a deal of making some money versus making none, the high volume salesman can be a good choice for you good barterers. Salesmen of the month receive more than those silly wall plaques. Money and free vacations are usually involved as prizes, so the more cars a good salesmen sells, the better his chances of winning. Even a small profit from your sale will put a notch on his sales number belt.

If you don't feel that your bartering skills are up to a match with the high pressure boys at the top of the sales charts, you might want to try a rookie. The turn-over rate for used car lots is exceptionally high, due mainly to the combination of high job pressure and low job status. Would you want to be in their shoes, having to sell used cars day after day, continuously being pushed by the manager? And being viewed by most people as someone to never trust who will tell any lies just to sell a car? I imagine you'd find this state of affairs a sorry one, and so do many of those who give it a try—in many used car lots the average salesman's stay is less than six weeks. This high level of personnel turn-over can be used to your advantage. The less experienced salesman will not have their sales techniques honed down as well as a seasoned pro. They might not have the stamina of a high level salesman, and they will often take a smaller commission in an attempt to sell any car. So you may be able to cut a better deal and use up less of your own precious time in the bargain. To spot a rookie salesman, take a general look around the salesmen's desk. Look for the man who has no sales award plaques hanging on the wall, and who isn't continually on the phone talking to customers. He may be younger in age than the other salesmen, but not necessarily. Some men try being a used car salesman after a previous career failed, so older men can also be sales rookies. Their sales techniques may often be rough and brash, but remember—you are there to buy a car, not to make a friend.

When you walk onto the car lot, don't be taken in by the first salesman who comes walking towards you with his hands just waiting to shake yours. Politely say that you want to just look around the lot ALONE first. Then FIRMLY tell him that you will ask for assistance when you need further information. Spend some of your time looking at the cars (even if you already know which model you want), but spend most of it checking out the salesmen. Pick out the man you feel will be best for you—don't let the salesman control the situation and pick you as a customer. If your instincts were wrong and you end up picking the wrong salesman, you can always pick another. Just be sure that it's you who does the choosing. Then give the bartering process your best shot.

The Bartering Process For Everyone.
Whether you're dealing with a private individual selling their own car or a professional salesperson, the bartering process itself hasn't changed since the olden days of horsetrading. The person selling the car has something you want (a car) and you have something they want (money). The only thing that complicates this basic deal is if you want to trade in your old car, and I will deal with that aspect later in this chapter. As the potential buyer, you can not show a great deal of enthusiasm towards the car, because it will lean the bartering scales towards the seller. Be rather bland, and tell the seller that you're looking for this sort of car, because you think it might be ok for your purpose. Give the seller an impression of someone who views cars as a necessary evil, a form of transportation to get from here to there.

If your chosen car has added luxuries such as power windows and a sun roof, show no interest in them. You can even turn the tables and mention how your last car had these extras, but that they were always breaking down and cost a fortune to repair. Conversely, if the car you're attempting to purchase is a base model car with little or no extra items, turn the tables. Mention how you're really looking for a car with more options, but that you might buy this car if the price is right. Always be in control of the bartering process—make it seem like you are doing the seller a favor by taking this used car off his/her hands.

ACT INDECISIVE THROUGHOUT THE BARTERING PROCESS Keep the seller on the edge of their seat, always wondering if you're going to buy the car or not. It may sound strange, but your indecisiveness will help you control the bartering. Act as if you're not sure this is the type of car you want—the color doesn't seem right; you really wanted a four door car; you're just not comfortable buying a car with so many miles on it; and so on. If you lean a little towards indecisiveness already, let your inhibitions loose and fire away at the seller. You and your mechanic have already decided that this car is fine—but the seller doesn't know this. Always keep them guessing, don't lay all your cards on the table for them to see.

Use the list that you and your mechanic have made of every single thing that was wrong with the car. Larger problems should take paramount position in your bartering, but even small ones can help tip the scales towards you (remember the straw that broke the camel's back). Show the seller your mechanic's repair estimates for these problems. Explain how these are just estimates and the actual cost may of course be larger. Since the seller has not bothered to repair these items, he/she should expect to get less for the car. Your seller may counter with the typical "these are just little things that don't cost much to fix". Then you just tell them how they should have fixed them before selling the car, unless they are willing to sell the car for less. As everyone knows, fixing things are easier said than done—many repair jobs become more complex and time consuming as the actual repairs are begun. Think of the time your bathroom faucet was dripping, and you thought a new plastic washer would solve all your problems. But after three trips to the hardware store, and hours of your own sweat (and perhaps an ensuing stream of profanities), the drip has turned into a raging waterfall. If you have a good mechanic, the repair process itself isn't going to end up like Niagara Falls—but don't let the seller know this. Show a little less knowledge here on your own behalf. Explain how you're never quite sure if car repairs have been done correctly, and are now rather ambivalent about the car. Remember that the bartering process is a GAME—you have already decided that this car is a good one, now you are trying to lower the price. Some people may be satisfied with a certain price rather quickly, and may not want to play the game any further. They can put their money down and drive away happy. But if you want to carve out the best deal possible, you've got to play the game hard. It's your money and why should you spend any more of it than you possibly have to? You're not here to make friends (or enemies for that matter), you're here to hammer out the best deal possible.

One of the best bartering aspects to use is the car's body and paintwork. Since you're looking at a used car, there are bound to be little scrapes, dents, or faded paintwork somewhere on the car. Cosmetic blemishes tip the bartering scales towards you for one simple reason—people are much akin to crows. Bright shiny objects attract them in ways that are often beyond logic. Every used car salesman knows that a shiny car will always sell for top dollar long before a faded one; even if the shiny vehicle is mechanically suspect and the faded car runs like a top. You can use this fact in your favor when purchasing a used car. Discover every single blemish that exists in the car's paint and bodywork, and use them for greater bartering leverage. Explain to the seller that you have had paint and bodywork done on some of your previous cars, and that the car was never quite right again. Either the body parts rusted later on, or the paint faded severely after a year or so. If you do know a good paint and bodywork shop, this poor workmanship isn't a worry. But good paint and body work does not come cheap. And this should be reflected in the price you pay for a blemished used car—even if you have no intentions of repairing the blemishes.

Perhaps you or your check out mechanic have discovered paint and bodywork on the car that has been done poorly, even though the car looks ok at first glance. Don't let this opportunity to lower the car's price pass you by. Explain to the seller that poorly done paint and bodywork is even more expensive to repair. In order for the job to be done correctly, the poorly done work has to be stripped off the car right down to the bare metal. As a personal example, I once purchased a car that had a rear door cheaply repaired with plenty of plastic bondo and incorrectly matched paint. I knew the repairs had been done cheaply, because I had told the owner to sell the car "as is" and not to pay for a cheap fix. But he ignored my advice and spent seventy five dollars on a very poor repair job. As fate would have it, he still couldn't sell the car for his asking price. When I purchased the car, I did so at a very good price—mainly because of the poorly done bodywork. When I had the car repaired correctly, my bodyman told me the car would have been much easier (and cheaper) to repair if it had just been left dented. The extra time taken to remove the poorly done work raised the cost by hundreds of dollars. Even if you plan on living with relatively poorly done bodywork, don't let the seller know. Use this to lower the car's price. Because no one knows what the future will bring. You may have to sell the car yourself in the future, and poorly done bodywork will be your problem the second time around.

To Trade Or Not To Trade—That Is The Question.

Speaking of the second time around, what are you going to do with your old car? For most people, the general agreement is "to trade is human, to sell divine". Selling your old car to someone else will always result in a higher selling price than trading it in at a lot. But are you and the car ready to go through the process of selling your own car? Here you need to make two judgement calls: 1. Is your car in good shape? And 2. Are you willing to spend time dealing with the public at large attempting to sell your car?

1. What type of shape is your car in? Is it on its last legs and just a few inches away from the junkyard? Is it in excellent shape? Or is it somewhere in between? Here you need to step back from your car and

attempt to view it objectively. Forget about all those great vacations you had in it, forget about the time you brought your new baby home from the hospital in it (let's not get maudlin), forget about having it bronzed. Cars are not horses and can't be put out to pasture. You need to look at your car objectively if you plan on selling it. (If you are rather eccentric, and plan on being buried in your Ferrarri like that rich woman was a few years back, you can skip this section.)

If your car is in good shape you should attempt to sell your own car. And if you are buying your "new" used car from a private individual, you will have to sell your old car if you want to get a decent amount of money for it. There are lots and wholesalers who will pay you cash for your old car, but they won't give you much. I once had a customer who was moving out of the country and had to sell her two year old car. She had waited too long, and only had three days left before setting sail. The car did have ninety five thousand miles on it, but they were all highway miles, since the car was only two years old. She only received fifteen hundred dollars cash from a used car lot. The lots know that most people will only sell their car to them as the last resort. Their price will always reflect this—they have you "over a barrel" and will take full advantage of this situation. If your car is in good shape, always attempt to sell it on your own. If it's really in bad shape or has quit running completely, you should think about scrapping it, or selling it for its various parts, or maybe even donating it to a charity "car smash" at the local demolition derby.

2. Are you willing to spend time dealing with the public at large selling your own car? As anyone who has ever dealt with the public will readily admit, it can can be a real bother at times. Be prepared to spend a chunk of your own time at this selling process. And speaking of preparation, get your car ready for the auction block. Clean it up inside and out, have it waxed and polished. Repair all the obvious things that may be wrong with it. A cracked side view mirror doesn't cost much to replace, and it will greatly enhance the car's appearance. If your car is still worth a good chunk of change, consider having the car and it's engine detailed by an auto detail shop. The hundred dollars or so you will spend may net you thousands in the long run (remember the crow analogy). And if the car's tires are in sad shape, you might consider purchasing a cheaper set at the local discount tire store. Don't waste your money on a a good set and pay for all the bells and whistles—like lifetime tire balancing and the road hazard insurance that most stores love to sell you at a premium. Just stick to the lowest price tire they

stock for your size rim. Most people view tire buying as a real hassle, so a nice looking set of tires on your car will make it that much easier to sell the car smoothly.

As it takes all kinds of people to make the world go round, you may have to deal with some of the shadier sides of humanity if you decide to sell the car on your own. Be prepared to deal with the people who want something for nothing—who will offer you ten cents on the dollar for your car. Be prepared to run into professional car buyers who plan on buying your car very cheaply and then just turn around and sell the car to somebody else at a huge profit. And be prepared to deal with those indecisive sorts who can never seem to make up their minds, and who may back out of a done deal five minutes before you are supposed to meet them at the bank. But don't be disheartened here—because if you decide to trade your car in, you will certainly be dealing with these type of people. A used car lot that takes trade-ins does so only to make a profit—they are professionals and certainly aren't going to cut you any slack. Most people on the street are much less knowledgeable about the true value of a car. You have a much better chance of cutting a good deal with a regular individual because of this. I have seen some of my own customers sell their old car for thousands of dollars more than their loan value. This would never happen when trading in a car at a used car lot (unless you were purchasing a car from this lot and were paying thousands more for the car than it was actually worth). As an example, Shelly was selling her four year old car because I had warned her about the many problems this particular model was having. Everyone involved in the car business knew about these problems, and wouldn't have given even a thousand dollars for the car. Shelly took my advice, and had the car detailed in and out. She also put a cheap set of new tires on all four wheels. Within two days of her advertising the car in the local paper, a couple came and bought the car for five thousand dollars. Admittedly, Shelly was a very good businesswoman; but she would never had gotten this amount of money unless she had sold the car herself.

If you really don't want to go through the bartering hassles yourself, for whatever reason, there is another approach you may want to try. There are many people out there who sell cars for other people on consignment. Used car brokers make a living by selling cars for other people—either by selling cars and taking a percentage of the sales price, or by charging a set fee for selling a car. These people are professional sellers, and can often sell a good car for top dollar. They have lists of people who are looking to purchase certain types of cars. If your car is one of them, they will certainly want to deal with you—that's how they make a living. They're basically middlemen in the selling process, they connect sellers with buyers. You may have a friend who has sold a car through one of these brokers—ask around. It's always better to deal with a car broker that you have some personal knowledge about, the same as you would with your mechanic. And you need to be very wary about lots that charge a set fee up-front before they sell your car. Some brokers will tell you that they charge five hundred dollars up-front to sell your car— especially if they are going to have the car sitting on their lot. This may leave them with little motivation to sell your car, because they already have your money. And even if they take this straight fee after the sale, it really isn't in your best interest. If the broker is getting a percentage of the car's selling price, this motivates them to sell the car for as high a price as possible. They are bartering not only for you, they are also bartering for their own profit margin. A percentage brokering deal is much more "above board" for everyone involved. In the used car game, salesmen should only be rewarded when they sell a car. If you reward them before a sale is finalized, you aren't playing by the rules. And you can just guess who ends up as the loser.

What To Do If You Absolutely Have To Finance Through The Seller.

Hopefully you have been able to borrow your car-purchasing funds from a source other than the car's seller. As previously discussed, expend a good deal of your own energy attempting to borrow the money from any source available. Bringing cash to the bartering process will give you a commanding position, and should allow you to cut the best price possible. But if you absolutely positively can not borrow the money elsewhere, here are some tips to keep the seller's claws from going too deeply:

1. Always let the salesman know that you are interested in only three basic things—the price you are paying for the car, the interest rate you are paying for the car, and how many months it will take to pay off the loan. (A fourth optional aspect would be the money you are getting for a trade-in, if you choose not to sell your old car on the open market.) DO NOT GO INTO A USED CAR LOT SAYING YOU WANT TO BUY A CAR WITH A MONTHLY PAYMENT OF X DOLLARS AND A DOWNPAYMENT OF Y DOLLARS. Every used car lot on the planet Earth is looking for such a customer. They can make any car on the lot fit your desired figures by simply raising the interest rate and the loan's length. As an example, I recently overheard a man in a local auto

parts store bragging how he got what he wanted out of a used car salesman. He was boasting how he had stuck to his figure of two hundred and fifty dollars a month, and five hundred dollars down. The salesman had wanted more, but he had not moved one inch. He purchased the car for his own original figures. So I inquired what type of car he had purchased, and he proudly gave me a tour of his new used car sitting outside in the parking lot. The car had a street value of perhaps fifty five hundred dollars—a customer of mine had recently purchased a similar model for five thousand dollars. But the man in the auto parts store will have paid ninety five hundred dollars for the car when his three years of payments are done. By sticking strictly to a given monthly payment and a set downpayment, he definitely got the wrong end of the stick. And you certainly don't want to join him.

By interplaying the car's selling price with the loan length and loan interest rate, salesmen can make your head spin with a veritable universe of differing figures. You control the situation by simplifying the process. Tell them you are only interested in the price you pay for the car, the interest rate you will pay on the loan, the length of the loan, and (if applicable) the money you will get for your trade-in. As I've previously discussed, you should already have a good base figure for the car's actual worth. You should barter first on the car's actual selling price, and then get into the nitty gritty of interest rates, loan length, downpayment level, and possible trade-in allowance.

2. Do not let the salesman pull the wool over your eyes with any of his old sales tricks—such as cash back, or a free first monthly payment. These will always be written right back into your monthly payment, and will often be reflected by a higher interest rate and/or loan length. Ditto for any extras that may be added on to your monthly payment—such as mandatory insurance policies that they may attempt to sell you. Find out what policies they are trying to sell you, and what such policies are going to cost you in total.

3. Do not attempt to barter the downpayment lower and lower. Try your best to come up with the biggest downpayment you can possibly afford. In all car deals (as in much of life), cash reigns supreme. By attempting to lower your downpayment, or by trying to eliminate it entirely, you are making your bartering control sink even faster. There are many car lots out there that will sell you a car for no downpayment at all. But you will end up paying three or four times what the car is actually worth, and your interest rate will probably be the highest that the law allows. By

financing a car through a used car lot, you have already put yourself in a very disadvantageous position—do not make it worse. Use the cash you have as a bartering wedge. It's your best tool here, so don't make it shrivel up by lowering the downpayment. Because if you do, you're playing right into the salesman's hands. He will be loaning you the lion's share of the deal, and he will control the bartering almost entirely. Your only real choice in the deal will be to sign on the dotted line, or to go and look elsewhere.

4. If you are planning on trading your old car in, assess the value of your old car exactly the same as you did for the car you want to purchase. Have a good idea what your old car is worth, and stick close to this value when you are talking trade-in allowance with the salesman. If your old car is in good shape, you won't get "street value" for it, but you should at least come close to its loan value. But remember my previous advice and barter over your new car's purchase price first. DO NOT ATTEMPT TO BARTER OVER YOUR TRADE-IN ALLOWANCE AND YOUR NEW CAR'S PRICE AT THE SAME TIME. Things will get too complicated, and you will play right into the salesman's hands. It means nothing if you have received a two thousand dollar allowance for your old clunker that wasn't even worth one thousand. Not if you are paying two thousand dollars above market value for your new car. If you feel unsure about your old car's value, take a few trial spins at different used car lots, and see what figures they come up with. Even if you don't see any cars on their lots that interest you, you can still get a decent average for your old car's trade-in value.

5. Do not get involved in the guarantee "racket" that many used car lots will attempt to lure you into. They will often attempt to keep the car's sale price high by offering various types of guarantees on the car. They may offer a thirty day guarantee on the car, or a fifty/fifty guarantee (where you pay half the labor and half the parts cost for repairs); or they may even offer to sell you an additional warranty policy on the car. All these guarantees have major flaws. In a fifty/fifty guarantee, just imagine what inflated repair figures your fifty percent will add up to! And just glance at the restrictions and non-covered items that any repair insurance policy contains. These policies really need a lawyer/mechanic blend to be understood, and they often contain wording that allows for a great deal of very different interpretations. You may feel a certain problem should be paid for by the policy, but if the company issuing the policy disagrees, guess who wins? Your best insurance policy is having a

good mechanic check the car out for you. Don't expect guarantees given by the used car lot to hold much water, and PLEASE, DO NOT SPEND YOUR OWN HARD EARNED CASH ON A CAR REPAIR INSURANCE POLICY. If you really feel you need that much insurance in your life, go out and spend a bundle on a brand new car and purchase a new car extended warranty policy. Then your money will be flowing away from you like a twig in a waterfall.

6. Be sure to tell the salesman that you want to see the car's odometer reading mileage statement. You certainly want to see it for the information it contains, but you also want to show the salesman that you're an informed consumer. If the statement is not from your local area (especially if it's from out of state), tell the salesman that this worries you quite a bit. You've read the newspaper articles and have seen the TV newsprograms that show the great deal of fraud that exists with out of state mileage statements. Of course your mechanic has already given the car his ok, but don't let the salesmen know this. Put the car in a negative light by this process, and see how much lower you can get the salesman to go—either in terms of the car's price or the financing interest rate.

7. Do not go into a used car lot with little or no knowledge of the prevailing used car interest rates. Shop around at a few lots, to see what type of financing rate you can get. If you find some lots are better than others for you, use this information as a tool. Maybe the lower interest lot doesn't have a car you want, but the other lots aren't going to know this. As an example, Janet was being quoted too high of an interest rate at Honest John's Used Car Lot. So she told John that Fred (of Fred's House of Happy Cars) will sell her a car for one interest percent lower. Janet made it very clear to John that she couldn't care less about where she purchased a car. She just wanted the best price and interest rate possible. So John eventually lowered his interest rate to make a sale, and Janet purchased the model she desired. A little knowledge can go a long way, and since you've chosen to finance a car through the lot, your main weapon is knowledge. Put it to good use, and barter the best deal you can.

8. Lastly, and perhaps most importantly, ACT INDECISIVE WITH THE SALESMAN THROUGHOUT THE ENTIRE DEAL. Being indecisive is extremely critical to the bartering process with a professional salesman. It is much more important to act indecisive in

front of a salesman than it would be if you were dealing with an individual selling their own car. The salesman makes his living selling cars on straight commission—he would much rather sell you a car for a smaller profit than not to sell you a car at all. Your indecisiveness can keep him on the edge of his seat, wondering if you are going to walk away and leave him empty handed. All used car salesmen live in fear of the "be-backers" who promise him they will return later—but who are never seen on the lot again. You need to keep the salesmen guessing throughout the entire bartering process by acting indecisive. If he starts worrying that you may soon turn into a be-backer, he will cut you a better deal for fear of losing you.

Bartering—The End Of The Line.

When you've ended the epic battle over the car's eventual sales price and the manner in which you're going to pay, it's time to wrap things up. If you're buying the car from a private individual, you need to receive the car's title, and have a simple receipt drawn up as follows:

I (name of seller)....... sell my 19.. (make and model)......(serial number)....... to (name of buyer)...... for (price of car).... on (date of sale).......... (signature of seller)......

Many states no longer even require that this statement be acknowledged by a notary public. If you're not sure about the laws in your own area, simply call up your bureau of motor vehicles and ask them what paperwork or possible forms are needed for a title transfer. Many areas now ask for proof of insurance before they will change the registration into your name—a phone call will give you all this information and save you a wasted trip.

Last Tips For Those Buying From An Individual

I've only got two more tips for those buying their car from a private individual:

1.Do not let your money change hands until both the car and its title are in your hands. If this necessitates a trip to the bank (to procure money or to view the seller's title that is being held by a bank), that is fine. But under no circumstances should you hand over your cash for either the car or the title alone. Future promises have a nasty tendency to go awry, and any honest deal will always involve your receiving both when money changes hands.

2. Do not drive away in your brand new used car without having the car insured beforehand. I have seen personal horror stories where my own customers were simply driving their newly purchased used car home. They hadn't bothered with getting any insurance yet, and the unmentionable happened. They were hit by an uninsured motorist, and their car was totalled. A simple phone call to your insurance agent can have your new car insurance begin at the day and hour you have decided to pick the car up. Your agent will certainly want to have you bring the car around within a few days to finalize the paperwork, but your car will be covered in the meantime.

Last Tips For Those Buying From A Lot.
   Before you sign on the dotted line at a used car lot, double check all the figures on everything you sign:

1. Make sure the car's serial number matches those on every form you must sign.

2. Be sure that the car's price (or amount to be financed) is the same that you have bargained for. Look very carefully for special add-on costs that they may attempt to sneak by you. Many lots will try to charge you for "car preparation" or attempt to add a "pick up fee" into the contract. If there are any fees on contracts, have them explained fully to you—and don't agree to pay them if they seem unwarranted to you. Tell them you can wax the car and fill it up with gas on your own. And if they are charging too high a fee for transferring the title and registration into your name, tell them you can handle the paperwork yourself. It isn't complicated at all—as long as the lot's title for the car is valid.

3. If you're buying your car's liability insurance from the lot, do some research on insurance rates beforehand. You should easily be able to get a better deal from an outside insurance agent. But if you can't, at least see what competitive insurance rates are. Don't let the lot sell you a policy that is at the top of the cost list. And for Heaven's sake, don't let them sell you some relatively expensive life insurance policy. Many lots will tell you that such policies are mandatory, so they will receive their finance money in case you suddenly expire. They also want to make the commission that goes with the policy. Check your local laws concerning this purchase of life insurance in conjunction with financing a car—it may or may not be a legal given. And even if it is, you'll get a much better price from an independent insurance agent. A life insurance

policy small enough to cover the cost of a used car would be extremely inexpensive. I've seen term life insurance policies for even 100,000 dollars cost my own customers less than 100 dollars a year. You can imagine how cheap a 10,000 dollar or less policy would cost. Even if you decide that buying more life insurance would be a good idea, a used car lot is certainly not the place to do so.

4. If you're financing through the lot, look at the finance percent rate on every paper you must sign. BE SURE if matches your agreed on figure. Once it's down on paper and signed, it's set in concrete—no matter what lower rate the salesman promised.

5. If you're financing through the lot, look at the amount of money the loan is for and the number of payments you will have to make. BE SURE these figures match those you've bartered for, and that no extra "hidden" payments have been added.

6. If there is a warranty agreement, read this carefully to assess what it may or may not cover. Again, what the salesman may have promised you means absolutely nothing. The lot will only hold themselves to what the warranty agreement contains. Even if you are getting no warranty from the lot, most areas have lemon laws that help protect the consumer from unscrupulous used car lots. If you are curious, look into them yourselves or contact a legal expert. They usually cover pre-existing conditions for the first month of ownership.

As an example, Francis purchased a car from Ted's Autorama. She knew little about the car buying process (unlike those who are almost finished reading this manual), and neglected to have a mechanic check the car out. One week later the engine stopped running, because the pistons had worn completely out. I examined the car and explained how she was looking at a great expense. Her best bet was to have a used engine installed, which would run about a thousand dollars. But I also told her about the local lemon law, and gave her the phone number of an attorney/customer of mine. After a few phone calls and a letter, the used car lot decided to install an engine free of charge. Certainly, this is the last option that anyone would want to pursue—but it's there as a last resort. A good check out mechanic is a much better choice—have him smell out the lemon before it ends up in your hands.

7. Lastly, do not pay your money until you have the car in your possession and it's in the exact shape that you've bartered for (be sure to

check the tires to make sure the lot hasn't pulled the old switcharoo trick of replacing good tires with bad ones). Keep any deposits low—the more money the lot is waiting on, the faster they will move to your commands. If the lot already has your money, you may discover that it will take forever to have that broken tail light assembly replaced, or to get that cracked windshield changed out. As usual in the car business, money screams—so don't lose your voice by handing the cash over prematurely. Use your last bit of leverage to ensure that nothing "funny" is tried by the lot.

AT LAST—YOU'VE GOT YOUR CAR.

Now that it's all said and done, you've got it—your brand new used car! You can take it for a leisurely drive in the countryside, you can rejoice over the money you've saved, you can even show it off to your mother. But what should you do to insure that it will give you years of faithful service? Why, just read the next chapter. It's for everyone—whether you plan on maintaining much of the car yourself, or just want to understand more about your car and how it should be maintained.

Chapter 6

A MECHANIC'S TIPS ON
MAINTENANCE AND LONGEVITY

Everyone wants their car to last Forever. We all dream of a car that runs trouble-free for 200,000 miles. I've seen many cars reach that vaunted goal, but it wasn't dreaming that got them there—it was good maintenance. Whether you are going to do the brunt of this maintenance yourself, or plan on having a professional mechanic do the chore, you need to make sure that your car is properly maintained. For those of you who plan on using a mechanic, unfortunately life is not as simple as it used to be. The days of my grandfather the local neighborhood mechanic have passed most of us by long ago. I'm sure there are still a few old-fashioned mechanics out there (I might even include myself as one of them). They can give you solid advice on maintaining your car correctly and will perform the task for a very reasonable fee. You can just hand your keys over to such a mechanic, and go your merry way—knowing that the job will be done right. But the old-fashioned mechanic is a dying breed, and the complexity of modern cars certainly has done much to finish them off.   The world is now full of chain repair shops, and large dealerships that have an immense overhead to pay for. The managers (or service writers) of these shops are paid commission percentages for every job that's sold to a customer. This is often a bad situation for you as the consumer—you may often be talked into maintenance work that your car really doesn't need. These shops have a high overhead and often spend a great deal of money advertising—and you can just guess who ends up paying for it all. In these modern times, you really need to know something about car maintenance and how often this maintenance should be performed on your particular car. You can't always trust that a shop will deal with you completely honestly—after all, they are running a business. Imagine if you walked into a designer clothes shop and asked the salesperson if you really needed to buy the outfit you noticed in the window. Do you seriously think they would say "no, you don't really need that expensive thing"? Many large repair shops will deal with you in the same manner—if you ask them whether your car needs a transmission service or not, they will certainly nod in the affirmative. You don't need to have a rocket scientist level of technical information shoved down your throat to keep things honest. But you should grasp a basic understanding of what maintenance procedures are crucial for extending the life of your car.

We've all heard the old saying, "If it ain't broke, don't fix it". This may apply to some aspects of your car (and to your own self as well), but it definitely does not apply to the following crucial maintenance items:

The Five Absolutely Critical Maintenance Items On Your Car.

1. Changing the engine's oil and filter.

The oil inside your car's engine performs two main critical functions—it lubricates the entire inner-workings of the engine, and it helps to cool down the immense heat generated inside the engine. Your car's engine is basically a machine that uses controlled explosions as a source of power. These explosions create a tremendous amount of heat, which must be removed or the engine will self-destruct. The explosions also result in a great deal of motion—even at forty miles an hour, your engine pistons may be going up and down two thousand times each minute. The friction created by this motion would melt the pistons down quickly if there was no oil serving as a lubricating barrier between metal parts.

Imagine yourself on a tropical island, bathing under a waterfall of crystal clear water. Think how good you'd feel being cascaded by its cooling spray. If your engine could talk, it would tell you how great it felt being sprayed by a nice clean supply of oil. But unfortunately for your car, its supply of clean refreshing oil gets dirty rather quickly. If our own supplies of fresh water became polluted as quickly as the oil in an automotive engine, we would indeed be in dire straights. Inside your car's engine, polluting elements begin to infiltrate the engine's oil supply soon after the oil is changed. Carbon soot, various acids, and other nasty byproducts of burning gasoline mix with the clean oil and begin to hinder the oil's effectiveness. After a certain period of time, the oil in your engine and its oil filter need to be changed. If it isn't changed, friction inside the engine will reach a threshold where the metal parts will begin to wear out Very Quickly.

IF YOU DO NO OTHER PREVENTATIVE MAINTENANCE ON YOUR CAR, AT LEAST CHANGE THE OIL REGULARLY.

I personally recommend changing the engine's oil and filter every three thousand miles (or twice a year if you drive very sparingly). Oil changes do not cost much money, and will do more to ensure the long life of your car than any other maintenance you can do to your car. Those who neglect changing their oil are saving pennies, only to lose thousands of dollars in the long run. An oil change may cost you around twenty dollars, but a new engine may cost four thousand dollars. And with the high tech nature of many late model cars, even repairing a dirty oil damaged engine (instead of replacing it entirely) can cost thousands of dollars. Engines with double overhead camshafts and four valves inside each cylinder (instead of the old two valves per cylinder) are very common in modern cars. They pollute less, they have more acceleration, and they get better gas mileage. But they are extraordinarily expensive to repair if they are damaged because of insufficient oil lubrication. You do not want to tempt fate with dirty oil in these engines.

As a real life example, Charley had his four year old car towed to me one morning. Upon cursory inspection of his car, I told him the timing belt in his engine had broken. His engine was making the distinctive sound engines make when their timing belts have snapped. So Charley gave me the go ahead to take apart the engine and replace the timing belt—about a three hundred dollar job on this particular model. When I dismantled the engine, the timing belt was indeed broken—but so was most of the engine. The cam shaft (that opens and closes the valves to let gas in and out of the engine) had broken completely in half. When I removed the oil drain plug on the bottom of the engine, not a single drop of oil came out! So I phoned Charley and asked him how he had been maintaining this car, as he was a brand new customer. He responded that the car was new to him—he'd just purchased it from his father. After getting his father's phone number, I gave it a ring to discover more about the car's past maintenance history. Charley's father said he'd been changing the car's oil "occasionally", and that the car had the most recent oil change sticker on the windshield. So I examined the sticker and discovered the oil had not been changed in sixteen thousand miles. As the car now had ninety thousand miles on it, I could only guess at how few times the oil had been changed. This lack of regular oil changes completely destroyed the car's engine. The engine had been so severely damaged, that repairing it correctly would have cost Charley more money than purchasing a brand new engine—which was bad enough at thirty-five hundred dollars. Fortunately for Charley, I found him a used engine in a salvage yard, and the whole job cost less than one thousand dollars. But that one thousand dollars would have bought him a few lifetimes worth of oil changes, and he wouldn't have had to deal with all the aggravation and inconvenience of a blown engine.

By changing your engine's oil and filter every three thousand miles (or twice a year if you are a low mileage driver) you won't become a cast member of such a horror story. But then you may well ask, "There are so many different types of oils and oil additives out there. Every manufacturer claims theirs is better than everyone elses. Which one should I use?" Things certainly seem to have gotten a little out of hand these days, with the proliferation of oil brands and oil additives presently on the market. There are non-detergent oils, detergent oils, synthetic oils, natural/synthetic oil blends, and a veritable mountain of oil additive products that are just screaming for you to buy them. If you are a normal driver, you just need to buy a good detergent engine oil and change it every three thousand miles, Period. Ask your mechanic which oil he recommends—there are many good brands out there that are competitively priced. High-tech synthetic oils and synthetic oil blends do last longer under extremely severe operating conditions, but their extra longevity and much higher price are not needed by the average driver. Any good detergent motor oil will keep your car humming along smoothly if you change it regularly.

As for the plethora of motor oil additives out there, they are not going to turn a worn-out engine into a new one. They may mask some engine problems for a short period of time, by thickening the oil that is in the engine—but they will not repair any real mechanical problems. If you do want to use these products for purely preventative maintenance, you can research the products out there and take your pick. I personally use one of those teflon oil coating additives once every 50,000 miles in my own cars for preventative maintenance. At around twenty dollars cost for every 50,000 miles, it's certainly cost effective. And I have seen some of my own customers who log over 200,000 miles on their cars swear by such oil treatments. But they also change their oil very regularly.

I ADVISE EVERYONE TO KEEP A SIMPLE LOG BOOK FOR THEIR CAR MAINTENANCE. YOU CAN BEGIN THIS LOG BY WRITING DOWN THE DATE AND MILEAGE OF EACH OIL CHANGE, AND WHEN THE NEXT OIL CHANGE IS DUE. It doesn't need to be anything fancy, even a fifty cent notepad stashed in the glove box would be fine. Just put it somewhere that is readily accessible, and remember to check it (or have your mechanic look at it) every couple months or so. It might seem like a silly thing to do, but it will come in very handy. Many of my own customers forget when their last oil change has been done, or how long ago it was since the radiator coolant was changed out. A simple little log book will ensure that your car is being maintained correctly. It will remind you when it is time to do important servicing, and will keep you from wasting your money doing ones which are not yet due.

2. Maintaining your car's cooling system.

The second most important aspect of maintaining your car is to keep the cooling system operating correctly. The intense heat created inside your car's engine would quickly cause a melt-down if the cooling system wasn't there—and maintaining this system is extremely simple. The coolant inside your car's radiator and engine block does not break down as quickly as the engine oil does. It merely needs to be flushed out and replaced once every three years! If you have just purchased a used car, I advise you to have the system flushed out and the coolant replaced soon after the car is in your hands. You can do it yourself with an inexpensive flush from any auto parts store, or you can have a professional mechanic do it for you. Either way, it's an inexpensive procedure that can add years of life to your car. Since most modern cars have plastic radiators with aluminum cores (instead of the older brass and copper style), this flushing is very critical for proper operating. The aluminum cores have a very nasty habit of becoming corroded when the antifreeze gets old and dirty. Everything will look fine to you (and to your mechanic) on the outside of the radiator, but the car will begin to run hotter as this corrosion builds up. The small amount of money you'll spend flushing the system out once every three years is definitely money well spent. Be sure to write this in your log book—who can remember to do something once every three years?

And while you (or your mechanic) are at it, inspect the various hoses for cracks and general old age. The cooling system is going to be empty anyway during the flushing process. You may as well change out the old hoses and clamps if they're looking poorly. Some fanatical maintenance people will change all the hoses out when they flush the cooling system. I personally think this is going a little too far, as I've had cars with original hoses on them that lasted well over ten years of hot Texas use. But if you're worried about the condition of the hoses, go ahead and change the main radiator hoses when you flush the coolant out. It won't cost much, and you can have peace of mind—especially if you're planning on taking the car for a long summer trip.

Before continuing on to the next crucial maintenance item, I have a very serious warning. DO NOT, UNDER ANY CIRCUMSTANCES, DRIVE YOUR CAR ONCE THE ENGINE HAS BEGUN TO OVERHEAT. If the temperature gauge reaches the H, or if the temperature idiot light comes on, or if steam begins to rise from under the car's hood—shut the car off immediately. Any car will be severely damaged if driven even a few miles with the cooling system inoperative. But modern day engines, with their extensive use of aluminum, will quickly become warped when overheated. In the olden days of cardom, most engines had cast iron blocks and cast iron heads. They were rugged and reliable, and could often take the immense heat created by a faulty cooling system without warping. You may even have once owned one of these cast iron behemoths, and drove it for a few miles while it was overheating. After having a blown hose replaced, you may have happily driven it away with no problems at all. But that would not be the case today—you would probably have warped many of the aluminum parts inside the engine. Depending upon the age and condition of your car, you could easily have to spend thousands of dollars—or give up completely and have the car towed to a junk yard. So always make a point of glancing at the temperature warning system of your car while driving, and pull over to the side if overheating problems arise. A small inconvenience now will greatly overcompensate for a huge, expensive inconvenience later.

As a sad example, John once towed his eight year old car to my shop. He said it had begun to overheat on the highway, and he decided to drive it three more miles to the next exit. While he was driving the car, it stopped running completely. I examined the car and spotted a broken water pump—about a hundred dollar repair job. But the engine itself had completely melted down inside. Although John's car was in immaculate shape, it ended up in the junk yard. It would have cost him more money to repair the intensive engine damage than it would have cost for a new engine—which was bad enough at over thirty-nine hundred dollars. A rebuilt engine would have cost him about two thousand, and even a used junk yard engine would have been about fifteen hundred when installed. A perfectly good car (with only sixty thousand miles on it) ended up in the junk yard because it was driven three miles while overheating. Don't follow in John's footsteps, no matter how inconvenient it may seem at the time. Shut off an overheating car and seek help immediately.

Of course, if you maintain your car correctly, you will keep yourself out of this situation in the first place.

3. Maintaining the car's automatic transmission.

Your car's automatic transmission contains fluid also. The car shifts gears through a combination of fluid pressure and electronic controls in modern cars. It is imperative that the fluid in the transmission remains clean—even a small amount of dirt can begin to clog up the tiny holes inside the transmission valve body. This can cause poor gear shifting, or even no shifting at all. Thankfully an automatic transmission is a sealed unit—dirt from the outside world can't enter as long as these seals remain intact (and these seals can often last hundreds of thousands of miles). And as the transmission doesn't have massive gasoline explosions occurring inside itself (like the car's engine), its fluid doesn't become contaminated very quickly from the inside either.

THE CAR'S AUTOMATIC TRANSMISSION FLUID AND FILTER (IF YOUR PARTICULAR MODEL CONTAINS A FILTER) ONLY NEEDS TO BE CHANGED AROUND EVERY 30,000 MILES. It's a very inexpensive procedure—and since it only has to be done so infrequently, be sure to write it down in your log book. If you need any further motivation, simply call up any auto parts warehouse that sells automatic transmissions. Ask them how much money a new, or even a remanufactured transmission would cost for your car. In many modern, computer controlled automatic transmission vehicles, this cost will run into the thousands. And I have personally seen people spend as much as two thousand dollars just to have their old transmission repaired at a transmission shop. So keep it clean and avoid having to deal with such problems.

A few car manufacturers may advise you to change it at slightly different intervals, but practically every automatic transmission car made will only need a change once every 30,000 miles. (The owner's manual will tell you if your particular model is different.) If your car manufacturer advises changing the fluid less frequently, I would advise you to ignore such advise and change it every 30,000 miles anyway. As a good warning example, car manufacturers a few years back were touting lower maintenance cars. They were telling people to change their engine oil only once every 9,000 miles on some models. In truth, they hadn't changed the reliability of their engines, they just decided that low maintenance was "in". So they told their customers to change their oil less frequently, magically making the car a lower maintenance car. I have seen engines in these 9,000 mile oil change cars wear out before their time, but of course it was after the warranty had expired. Changing the transmission fluid and filter every 30,000 miles is the best transmission warranty you can have. It's inexpensive and can even be done easily yourself—if you don't mind getting your hands a little oily.

If your car has a standard transmission, things are even simpler. The fluid in a standard transmission serves only to cool and to lubricate the transmission gears and bearings. It is just a simple splash lubrication system—there is no oil pump or small holes for the fluid to pass through. There is no filter to be changed inside the transmission. You only have to change the fluid in a standard transmission once every 50,000 miles or so. Your owner's manual will give you the figure for your particular vehicle—and unlike the case of automatic transmissions, if the manual says to change it less frequently, that's perfectly ok. It isn't a very critical maintenance factor in a standard transmission car.

4. Changing your car's timing belt.

Most cars today have timing belts inside them. You can't see them because they're inside the engine—but believe me, they are there. The timing belt physically connects the engine's crankshaft to the engine's camshaft(s). It allows the camshaft(s) to turn, opening and closing the engine's valves. If these valves do not open and close at very precise moments, the car will not run. Unfortunately for the consumer, car engines used to have metal timing chains instead of these more fragile rubber/fiberglass timing belts. The chains were rugged and reliable, and required very little maintenance at all. But they had one major drawback—they were expensive to make. The chains had to be enclosed in their own sealed oil supply, and the cogs that they ran on had to be made of very strong metal. The car engineers may tell you that these chains were replaced in order to make the car lighter and more gas efficient—but they really aren't telling the truth. The loss of less than five pounds of weight in a car that may total 2,500 pounds is hardly going to make much difference in gas mileage. The real reason for using timing belts (unfortunately for you) is that they are much cheaper to build. The belts themselves require no lubrication, so they don't need a sealed oil supply—which costs money to build. And since these belts are made of rubber and fiberglass, the cogs that they drive can be made of much cheaper metal alloys—or even made of plastic. Unfortunately this design seems to be here to stay, so you have to be aware of the very serious maintenance that they require. You certainly don't want to throw away your engine when it breaks, like you would with a cheap modern day appliance that's broken down.

THE TIMING BELT SHOULD BE REPLACED AT REGULAR STIPULATED INTERVALS—USUALLY EVERY 50,000 MILES. So at least it's something you don't need to do very often. Your owner's manual will tell you how often your particular model needs to be changed, or you can have your mechanic look it up for you. Unless you have a rather exotic car, it should only cost two or three hundred dollars. Those with exotic cars will just have to cringe—some Porsches routinely cost fifteen hundred dollars to have their timing belts changed out.

Here you may ask, what happens if I don't change the timing belt at the stipulated mileage? Well, that depends on the design of your particular car—something that you should find out from your mechanic (or other knowledgeable person). Some cars have engines with pistons that go up very high and valves that go down very low. If their timing belt breaks when the engine is running, the valves will hit the pistons and very serious damage will result. Other cars have engines which are better designed, and no damage at all will result when the timing belt breaks. As an example, I have seen Toyota Camrys that went 120,000 miles before the timing belt broke—even though Toyota recommends changing the belt every 60,000 miles. The engine on this particular car was not damaged at all—only the timing belt needed to be changed. But if the car had been a BMW, in all probability pistons and valves would have been damaged. The repair bill could easily reach three thousand dollars.

YOU NEED TO DISCOVER WHICH TYPE OF ENGINE YOUR CAR HAS IN IT—WHETHER YOUR ENGINE WILL BE DAMAGED INTERNALLY IF THE TIMING BELT BREAKS, OR WHETHER NO DAMAGE WILL BE DONE.

If your car has an engine which is not damaged when the timing belt breaks, you will only be inconvenienced if the belt breaks while you're driving the car. If you spend most of your time driving locally in a non-damaging timing belt car, you may want to wait on changing the timing belt until it breaks. Then just have your car towed to your mechanic and have a new timing belt installed. I have had quite a few of my own customers go this route. Sometimes their timing belts haven't broken until 120,000 miles—so they ended up paying for only one timing belt change instead of the two that the manufacturer suggested. And if they were going on a long trip and they were long past the suggested change mileage, they would often decide to have me change the belt before their trip. A small local inconvenience can easily become a major pain if it occurs while on vacation in a strange place with unknown mechanics. It's certainly been the main plot line of countless B horror films—although I doubt that you will be attacked by brain-eating monsters if your car conks out on some deserted country road.

But if your car has an engine that's damaged when the belt breaks, you're now stuck in the middle of a real horror show. The cost of engine damage can easily reach thousands of dollars. This serious damage often results in the car's last trip—a tow truck ride to the junkyard. Every car that has an engine which is damaged when the timing belt breaks should be maintained strictly according to the mileage figures given by the manufacturer. If they tell you to change the belt every 40,000 miles, change it every 40,000 miles. And conversely, if they say to change it every 80,000 miles, change it then. And as a special note, some cars that have damage causing timing belt designs also have water pumps that are driven by those very same belts. If the water pump breaks, the belt will snap and engine damage will result. Find out from your mechanic if your car is one of these vehicles—and if he tells you to change the water pump when the belt is changed, do so. Don't attempt to save a few dollars when doing such a crucial piece of maintenance. Have the job done correctly and you won't have to think about it for another 50,000 miles or so.

5. Maintaining the car's braking system.

The last of the critical maintenance items on your car is the braking system. You certainly want your car to have plenty of get up and go— but your car's stopping power has to be even greater. It's nice to have a car that accelerates like the wind, but it's crucial to have one that stops on a dime. A speeding car that can't stop quick enough in emergency situations is a potentially deadly one for anyone inside or outside the car. Think of your own driving experiences when a set of good brakes saved you from trouble. Then compare this with times that you absolutely had to accelerate quickly to stay out of trouble. If you're being honest, the screeching brake experiences will greatly outnumber the pedal to the metal ones. An overliberal use of the accelerator pedal will often create problems, not solve them.

As previously discussed, the braking system of your car transforms the tremendous kinetic energy of your speeding car into heat. It turns a potentially deadly speeding object into a safe motionless one. Modern braking systems have become so strong and reliable that they are usually taken for granted. They are much more powerful than their predecessors of even fifteen years ago, and at the same time they are designed to last longer. But like any machine, they do need maintenance if you want them to perform best and last longer. You don't want to wait until your car's brakes have completely broken down before you have them fixed. It would needlessly create dangerous situations, and in all probability it would end up costing you much more money—as the following example illustrates. Charley towed his three year old car over to me, because its brakes had gone out completely. He admitted that strange noises had been coming from the brakes for quite some time, but the car had been stopping ok. So he waited for them to have "a real problem" before having them checked out. Luckily for him, they brakes went out in his suburban neighborhood on a Saturday afternoon—not in rush hour traffic on a highway overpass. When I pulled off the wheels to inspect the damage, the right front wheel wobbled like mad. Charley had driven the car until the brake system had worn down to bare metal, and had destroyed over five hundred dollars worth of brake and suspension parts. If he had brought the car over when he began hearing strange noises, a simple brake job would have cost him around ninety dollars. Now he was looking at a six hundred and fifty dollar job (with labor included). You certainly don't want to be in Charley's shoes, so you should become better acquainted with your car's braking system and how to keep it properly maintained.

Unlike other aspects of car maintenance, your car's braking system has no definite mileage or time period in which maintenance needs to be done. You want to change your car's engine oil every three thousand miles and you want to flush the cooling system out every three years— but your braking system maintenance is not directly related to mileage or time. It's mainly dependent on you and how you drive your car. I have two different customers who drive the same exact model of car, but their frequency of brake repairs are radically different. Fred is a hard-charger who takes off like a rocket from every stop light, while Joe drives like the stereotypical "old man". I have to replace Fred's brake pads on a regular basis, sometimes as frequently as every fifteen thousand miles. But slow poke Joe is another story, he once went over a hundred thousand miles on a set of brake pads.

Although most people are somewhere inbetween the rabbit and the turtle in their driving habits, this does show you that braking wear and tear is mainly related to how you drive your car. Those who drive predominantly highway miles are going to have brakes that last longer. While those driving mainly in the daily grind of city stop-and-go traffic should expect their brakes to wear out faster. Those who drive faster will tend to wear their brakes out quicker than those who drive at moderate speeds. And those who drive with one foot always on the brake pedal will wear their brakes out quickest of all. (Believe it or not, there are still quite a few people out there who drive with one foot resting on top of the brake pedal—I have personally repaired these cars over and over again.)

So you may well ask, when should I have my brakes serviced? If you have access to a good mechanic, you can just have the wheels pulled off and the car road tested once every year or so when some other maintenance is being performed. It takes only a few minutes to have the brake lining thicknesses checked, and to eyeball the system for possible fluid leakage. And a good road test to finalize the brake check only takes your mechanic five minutes. If you're taking my advice and have a little notebook maintenance log in your glove box, you can just jot the mileage and date down for each brake check. And please take a serious note of caution here—DO NOT DEPEND UPON YOUR YEARLY SAFETY INSPECTION STICKER PROCEDURE TO GIVE YOU A GOOD BRAKE SYSTEM CHECK. All four wheels are never pulled off and checked—you will rarely get a serious thorough check out of your braking system during these inspections. And you may easily be taken for a repair ride that your car doesn't need if the inspection garage isn't being honest. I've had more than one customer who came to me worrying about brake repairs that inspection stations told them they needed to pass inspection. But in reality their cars had no brake problems at all. All honest mechanics detest these "bad seeds", as they give the trade a very bad name. If you ever find yourself dealing with such a dishonest inspection mechanic, please contact your local government authorities, as they are in charge of the inspection process. And don't hesitate to call the Better Business Bureau and fill out a complaint.

Finding an honest mechanic and dealing with them on a regular basis is your best policy for all car maintenance—but it's of paramount importance when you're dealing with your car's brakes. But if you don't know of one presently, a little brake knowledge on your own behalf can go a long way. You've probably been driving cars for quite some time, and you have a pretty good feel of your own car's braking system. You know when the brakes feel right—the car will stop in its normal fashion when you apply the normal amount of push on the brake pedal. If you find the pedal is getting mushy, or if it's going completely down to the floor, you know something isn't right. Or if the brake pedal becomes extremely hard to push down, you know it's time to have the brakes looked at. So the general rule of brake maintenance is as follows: IF THE BRAKES FEEL NORMAL AND STOP THE CAR FINE, THEY DON'T NEED TO BE REPAIRED—UNLESS THEY ARE MAKING LOUD NOISES.

Only here you may ask, what exactly is a loud brake noise? Is it a steady chirping like a bird, or more like the roaring of a lion? Unfortunately things are not as simple in the car braking noise department as they used to be (but then again, what is in these hectic modern times?). Due to health concerns, the use of asbestos in brake linings has been made illegal. Asbestos is a hard compound that can take great amounts of heat without any damage. It was especially useful in car's braking systems because it would last for a long time and didn't make noises when the brakes were applied. Today many other materials have been used to replace the asbestos, and many of these new materials last much longer than the asbestos linings did. But unfortunately many of these new materials are rather noisy. It is very common amongst later model cars to hear strange noises come and go when the brakes are being applied. High pitched squeals, low pitched groans, and even sometimes rather hellacious grinding type noises will often occur in some cars with these non-asbestos brake lining systems. Brake noises in these cars do not necessarily mean that you need to have your brakes repaired—especially if the noises are not occurring every time you use the brakes.

Relatively random brake noise can be rather common in these cars, with the noise level intensity being dependent upon a rather complicated set of factors. If the humidity level is very high, these new linings may get a thin layer of rust on them which will cause noise (especially first thing in the morning). If it is extremely cold outside, the linings may make quite a racket until they have been warmed up. To compensate for this added noise factor of these new types of brake linings, car makers have installed a brake lining warning system into many new cars. In higher priced luxury cars, there is an electric warning system that tells you the linings are thin and need to be replaced. And in most other modern cars, there is a metal "squealer" built into the linings themselves. When the linings get thin, the metal squealer begins to rub against the brake rotor. This noise is a constant noise that appears every time you apply the brakes—it's telling you to have the linings replaced. And if you've driven your car for a few miles with the squealer sending out its warning, the noise may even stay on after you've taken your foot off the brake pedal.

It's a good idea to have your brakes checked when you hear a bothersome constant noise coming from the braking system. Even if your mechanic pulls off the car's wheels and shows you that the linings are not worn out, you haven't wasted your time. Because you will have learned that such noises are nothing to worry about in your car. And the more knowledge you have about your car's brakes, the better you will be able to fend off possible "rip-off" repairmen. Contrary to the many TV advertisements for nationwide brake repair shops, very few of their customers will be told that those strange sounds coming from their brake systems are normal. Once inside many of these shops, high pressure sales techniques will be used in an attempt to overwhelm you. If you think your car's braking system may have a problem, I seriously doubt if they will attempt to convince you otherwise. Most managers are on a commission bonus salary—they view you driving away without purchasing anything in the same vein as money flying out of their pockets. A little knowledge on your behalf can give you peace of mind and keep you away from this repairland spider web.

A Special Note On Anti Locking Brake Systems.
The last note here on maintaining your car's braking system has to do with ABS systems. ABS stands for anti-locking braking system. This system keeps your wheels from skidding during harsh or slippery braking situations. Quite a few new cars contain ABS brakes, and it's a good idea to find out whether your particular car has them. If your car does have ABS brakes, it would be a good idea to perform one small bit of extra maintenance on your car's brakes. You should have the fluid in your brake system flushed out and replaced with new fluid every two years or so. Some manufacturers have suggested that this flushing and replenishment be done on all their cars, but I feel this is going a little too far (unless you drive your car in a very corrosive environment such as a salt water coastal area). ABS braking systems have many extremely small ports and valves that the brake fluid must pass through. Even an almost infinitesimal bit of corrosion in the brake fluid can cause malfunctioning of an ABS system. Flushing out the brake system every two years or so is a wise precaution to take. As ABS systems are computer controlled and most repair parts are available only through car dealerships themselves, the cost of repairing these systems can be very high. There are little (if any) aftermarket repair parts available for ABS systems, so the dealers often charge extravagant prices for even the smallest items. The insignificant cost of flushing out ABS brake systems every two years is a true bargain when compared to the great expense of repairing a broken system.

The Other Maintenance Items On Your Car.
By performing the previously discussed five critical maintenance items on your car, you will help your car last as long as possible. And you'll have peace of mind knowing that your car will not have major problems that could have been prevented with only a small amount of time and money. Now I'll discuss other maintenance items that are not as critical, but which can be easily checked and can further the reliability and lifespan of your vehicle.

A. Your Car's Fuel System.
Your car's fuel system consists of the fuel tank at one end of the car and either a carburetor or a fuel injection system at the other end. Inbetween them are the fuel lines that carry the fuel, a fuel pump or pumps to push the fuel along, and a fuel filter or filters to keep

impurities from reaching the engine. In the olden days of cardom, every car had a simple mechanical fuel pump and a rather primitive carburetor to deliver the air/fuel mixture inside the engine. The pump would only deliver a tiny two pounds of fuel pressure to the carburetor. The carburetor would use this small fuel pressure in combination with a small amount of engine vacuum pressure to mix the fuel with air and spray this mixture into the engine. Many of the older cars didn't even have fuel filters in them to take out impurities. If something went awry with the fuel system, an old-time mechanic would just open up both ends of the fuel system and blow the dirt out with air.

But today most car's are fuel injected. They may even have two fuel pumps to deliver a fuel operating pressure of seventy-five pounds per square inch. They can have two separate fuel filters to ensure that no impurities reach the fuel injectors. And the fuel injection system itself is certainly controlled by one or more ECU units (or computers in layman's terms). Modern fuel injected cars have reached a level of complexity that wouldn't have been dreamed of fifty years ago. Many people often complain about problems relating to this complexity—they see their car are being so complicated that no one can figure out how to repair it. Now I must admit that there are a few luxury car models out there that seem to have been designed by engineers who were on the tail end of a drunken spree. But most modern fuel injected cars are infinitely more reliable than their carburetored predecessors. They operate more efficiently, they allow the engine to put out more horsepower, and they can go much longer between servicing. A well designed fuel injection system allows an engine to run at its peak level of efficiency for a very long time.

You certainly want your fuel system to perform at its peak, so what should you do to maintain it? Basically, you just need to do two simple things: 1. Fill your car up with good gasoline. 2.Change your fuel filter(s) regularly to ensure no dirt enters the injectors or the carburetor. As long as you fill your car's fuel tank with a good grade of fuel, you will keep nasty things from happening to your car—like wheezing, jerking, or stalling. But what exactly is a good grade of fuel for your car? Fortunately, this is simpler to discover today than it used to be. Due to various underground water anti-pollution laws, most of the old rusting gasoline underground storage tanks have been dug up and replaced with fiberglass underground tanks. And all the new tanks being installed have to meet exacting standards. Not only does this keep gasoline from polluting ground water supplies, but it also ensures that your car's fuel system does not get polluted with rust, water, or other impurities. Bad gas resulting from older, leaking tanks is not something that happens very often anymore—which is good news for you.

Then you may ask, what brand of gasoline should I buy? This depends partially on personal preferences (especially if you happen to work for an oil company), but I can give you a simple rule of thumb. Find the gas station nearest your home, and purchase a tank of the lowest price gas they have. If your car runs fine, and doesn't make any pinging noises when the engine is accelerating hard, that level of gasoline is fine. If it does ping, try the second price level. And if your car still pings, try the third, and highest level of gas that they sell. If you car is still pinging with the highest level of gas, you need to have your car serviced—or you need to try gasoline at a different brand of station. Most cars today will run fine on regular, and don't need the higher octane more expensive fuel. Some luxury or sports cars with souped up engines require the higher level of fuel, as do many older cars which were designed for higher octane levels in fuel. You may have to buy the most expensive level of fuel for these cars if you want them to perform correctly. But as long as your car's engine does not ping when accelerating, whatever level of fuel you buy is fine .

The other basic maintenance you can do for your car's fuel system is to regularly have the fuel filter(s) changed. Fuel filters are not very expensive, so FOLLOW THE SUGGESTED CHANGING PERIOD THAT YOUR PARTICULAR MANUFACTURER SUGGESTS IN THE OWNER'S MANUAL—IT'S THAT SIMPLE. If you wish to be extremely cautious, have your fuel filter(s) changed once a year (especially if you happen to have neighbors with children who have a nasty habit of putting foreign objects in other people's gas tanks).

A Special Note For Those With Diesel Cars.

Diesel cars are fueled by diesel (it certainly doesn't take a genius to figure that one out). Unlike gasoline, diesel is not an extremely caustic liquid—believe it or not certain molds and funguses can actually thrive inside a diesel fuel tank. Those of you with diesel powered cars have to be even more careful about your fuel supply and its filtering system. It's a very good idea to put an anti-fungal fuel additive into diesel fuel tanks three or four times a year. This will prevent the growth of mold and fungus that would clog up the diesel injection system. And it would be a good idea to change your fuel filter(s) once a year. Many people with diesels opt to add an additional fuel filtration system—there are many available for around a hundred dollars, and they are very easy to install. If you don't take your diesel car on long trips, or if you let it sit unused for any length of time on a regular basis, I would advise you to install one of these additional filtration systems.

B. Having Your Car "Tuned Up".

In the old days of cardom (sometimes as far back as twenty years ago), having your car tuned up was a regular feature of car maintenance. The ignition system was controlled by mechanical parts that would physically break down after as little as ten thousand miles of use. And the carburetors of these cars would often need quite a bit of tinkering to keep the car running smoothly. But today's modern computer controlled cars operate much differently. Their sophisticated electronics are actually "tuning up" your car hundreds of times each second. Their ignition systems are either distributors with magnetic fields (which have no friction and don't wear out over time) or are entirely computer based and have no moving parts to wear out. And their fuel injection systems are also computer controlled and have little, if any, moving parts that need constant replacement. Some car manufacturers have even begun advertising that their car's first suggested tune up isn't until the car has reached 100,000 miles.

So what about the good old tune up that everyone seems to want for their car? You see advertisements everywhere proclaiming $59.95 tune ups—but what exactly are you getting, and do you really need it? In most of these discount "tune ups" you're going to get a new set of spark plugs, period. Everything else is just inspecting parts of the car. Since many new cars use advanced spark plugs with a very long life span (some platinum plugs can last 100,000 miles), you may not even need new spark plugs. The day of the car tune up has really been passed by, and replaced by regular servicing. This emphasizes the importance of keeping a car maintenance log for your car. You just need to write down all your car servicing in your log, so you (or your mechanic) will know the car is being serviced correctly. As long as you maintain your car as I describe in this chapter, and write down all this servicing in your log, your car will not need periodic "tune ups". The spark plugs in the engine can be quickly checked and replaced if needed when other servicing is being done.

C. Your Car's Front End And Steering Systems.

The front end system of your car keeps your wheels firmly on the ground and allows you to steer your car. In the olden days, this system had various grease fittings and bearings that needed to be greased and lubricated. When you had your engine oil and filter changed, you would also have the car's suspension system greased. But aside from a few very expensive luxury cars and some four wheel drive sport utility vehicles, cars no longer have grease fittings or greaseable bearings on them. These parts are self-lubricating and are sealed systems. The ball joints, tie rods, and wheel bearings in most cars today require no maintenance. (If you want to discover if your car is one of the rare cars that does need greasing, ask your honest mechanic. And if he says you do, be sure to write this down in your maintenance log.) The only thing you need to do to ensure their long life is to miss most large objects in the road (such as curbs and blocks of cement that have fallen off the back of the truck in front of you). You wouldn't want to bend or break any of these parts inadvertently.

Those who want to be extremely cautious can have an honest mechanic check the front end alignment once every two years, to ensure that the front end is perfectly adjusted. But for everyone else, wait until you notice problems occurring in the front end before you start spending money. If your car's steering wheel is starting to give you the shakes, or is beginning to pull to one side (especially if your car has recently hit a large pothole or other foreign object) have a good front end mechanic check it out then.

The steering system in modern cars is also a sealed system that is virtually maintenance free. If your car has manual steering, there are really no service adjustments that are needed to keep the system working smoothly. And if your car has power steering, the only thing your need to do for maintenance is to have the power steering fluid changed out once every three years or so—a very inexpensive procedure. In cars that are getting a little long in the tooth (being more than five years old), you or your mechanic can check the power steering fan belt, the power steering rubber hoses, and the power steering rack boots for cracks or possible fluid leakage. If your power steering system is beginning to leak, you will hear the power steering pump groan when the wheel is turned. This means that the power steering fluid is below a safe level. You should add more fluid and have the system checked out when this happens. And as a special note, BE SURE TO USE THE PROPER POWER STEERING FLUID FOR YOUR PARTICULAR CAR—DO NOT USE AUTOMATIC TRANSMISSION FLUID. In the past, most people viewed automatic transmission fluid as interchangeable with power steering fluid. But today's modern cars have different systems that can be seriously damaged if transmission fluid is used in place of the proper power steering fluid. Admittedly, automatic transmission fluid is cheaper, and most power steering systems will seem to operate ok if transmission fluid is put in them. But such fluid can begin to eat away at the power steering system's seals, and can cause very extensive (and expensive) damage. The few dollars more you'll pay for proper power steering fluid is well worth it.

D. Your Car's Drive Axle(s).

Your car's drive axle is what transmits the engine's power to the wheels that push the car. Cars either have one or two drive axles, depending upon their design (except for four wheel drive vehicles which can have five separate drive axles). In the olden days, practically every car was a rear wheel drive design, where the car only had one drive axle. It was known as the drive shaft, and it had grease fittings in its universal joints. An extremely small amount of cars today do have greaseable drive shafts. If you have one of these rare cars, be sure to have the joints greased when oil changes are being performed. But even most rear wheel drive cars today have sealed drive shaft universal joints, so they require no maintenance.

The vast majority of cars out there today are front wheel drive machines. These cars have two drive axles—one for the left front tire, and one for the right. There is a constant velocity joint at each end of both drive axles—making a total of four joints for the entire car. These joints are lubricated by a special molybdenum grease, which is sealed inside the joint by a rubber boot (or CV boot). These boots bend and twist as the drive shaft spins the car's wheels. Eventually, these boots become old and start to crack. The spinning of the drive axle then rips the boots open, and the joint's lubricating grease is thrown on the bottom of the car. With their lubricating grease gone, the CV joints begin to wear out. This wear will not be noticed by the car's driver until it is too late and the joints begin to make a clacking noise. This metallic clacking noise will first be noticeable when the steering wheel is turned far to one side or the other. As the car begins to turn hard, the clacking noise will be heard. This means that the joint's internal metal parts are wearing out, and the joint itself will need to be repaired. And in some models of car the joints themselves can not be repaired because of their design—the entire drive axle has to be replaced as a unit. Either way you are looking at a relatively expensive repair bill. IF YOU HEAR A LOUD CLACKING SOUND COMING FROM THE FRONT OF THE CAR WHEN YOU MAKE HARD TURNS LEFT OR RIGHT, IT'S TOO LATE—YOUR DRIVE AXLE HAS ALREADY BEEN DAMAGED.

But you can prevent such large repair bills with a very simple check. You (or your mechanic) can check the CV boot's condition whenever the engine oil is being changed. Just look at the ends of each drive axle. In front wheel drive cars, the outer CV boots are located just inside the left and right front tires. These outer CV boots are the most strained parts of the drive axle—they have to twist and bend severely when hard turns are made. They are inevitably the first boots to rip open and lose their grease. I have seen outer CV boots rip in cars that had around 50,000 miles on them—but the inner CV boots in these same cars would often last well over 100,000 miles. (The inner CV boots are at the other end of the drive axle from the outer CV boots. They are called the inner boots because they are closer to the inside of the car.) The actual mileage that CV boots last is dependent upon many variables—such as how many years old the boots are, the corrosiveness of their driving environment (salt water shortens their lifespan), the temperature of their operating environment (extremely hot or cold weather can age them quickly), and other factors too numerous to mention. So it's not a bad idea to check them occasionally. Once you have discovered there whereabouts on your particular car, it only takes a minute to check all four CV boots. It's a good rule of thumb to check them at every oil change, just to ensure they are being regularly inspected. Unless your time is worth three hundred dollars a minute (or even more if you have a luxury model with non-repairable drive axles), this small check is certainly worth your or your mechanic's attention.

E. Having Your Engine's Valves Adjusted.

In the old days, automotive engines needed their valves adjusted constantly—sometimes as often as every five thousand miles. But thanks to advances in modern metallurgy and engine design, this constant attention is a thing of the past. Many car engines use a hydraulic lifter design, where the valves are automatically adjusted through engine oil pressure. As long as you change your oil regularly, you will be maintaining the valve adjustments correctly—the hydraulic lifters adjust the valves as you drive.

If your particular car has an engine that does have manually adjustable valves, abide by the mileage figures that the manufacturer suggests. It may be once every thirty thousand miles, or once every fifty thousand miles—just be sure to have the valve adjustments checked at the mileage the manufacturer suggests. If you've lost the owner's manual, just ask your mechanic. If he doesn't know it off the top of his head, he can easily look the figure up. Unless you own a rather exotic luxury car, having the valves adjusted it not a major expense. Valve adjustment is a critical factor in correct engine performance, because

incorrect valve adjustment can lead to severe internal engine damage—
bent valves, broken engine heads, and overheating engines. But you
should not lose any sleep over this, because most modern day engines
are strongly built. The engines being built today often will not go out of
adjustment for well over 100,000 miles. YOU SHOULD ALWAYS
HAVE YOUR ENGINE VALVE ADJUSTMENTS CHECKED AT
THE MANUFACTURER'S SUGGESTED MILEAGE—BUT THEY
MAY NOT NEED TO BE ADJUSTED. I have personally checked
hundreds of engines for correct valve adjustments at the manufacturer's
suggested mileage, and discovered that few of the valves had worn out of
adjustment. I have even owned cars with over 100,000 miles on them
that had never gone out of adjustment. I checked the valves every fifty
thousand miles in these cars, but I never actually had to adjust a single
valve. It's certainly better to be safe than sorry—so have your valves
checked at the stipulated mileage (if your car doesn't have hydraulically
adjusted valves). But you or your mechanic may not have to purchase
any valve adjusting parts (such as valve shims or rocker arms), because
they may not need any adjustments.

F. Your Car's Tires.

The tires on your car are very simple to maintain. Simply have their
air pressure checked occasionally, perhaps once a month or so. As
modern times have created a self-service society, don't expect anyone to
do it correctly for you. Just go out and purchase either a tire pressure
gauge, or one of those foot air pumps that has an air gauge built in. The
reason I suggest an air pump with a built in gauge is because you may
not be able to find an operating air pressure hose ANYWHERE. If you
don't mind doing the pumping yourself, you will be assured of an air
pressure supply. And besides, if you are in the middle of nowhere and
discover that one of your tires is going down, you can just take your
trusty air pump out of the trunk and save yourself.

Just keep your tires at the correct pressure—usually about twenty
eight pounds per square inch, when the tires are cold. Tire pressure goes
up when the car is driven and the tires heat up. Some tires use a
different range of pressure, so be sure to ask your mechanic or tire
company what exact pressure you should be using.

If you're really into your car's tires, you can spray and buff them
endlessly with any of those new tire polishing sprays that everyone
seems to be selling today. They won't really add much lifespan to your
tires, but they make them look nice and shiny. And if you're really into
tires, you can inspect them often for little cuts and signs of uneven

120

wear—but please don't become neurotic about them. I've seen countless examples of the proverbial "old man" checking out his tires and picking all the little pebbles out of the tire tread. Please don't join that group— the stones will just return as soon as the tires start moving again— though the neurosis may last forever.

G. Your Car's Electrical System.

Today's cars are controlled by very sophisticated computer systems, but their basic power supply hasn't changed much from the early days of cars. A twelve volt battery is used to start the car, and an alternator is used to recharge the battery and supply extra electrical power for running the car.

Your car's battery.

There are various types of batteries available today, but almost every car out there has a sulfuric acid battery under the hood (or in the trunk, or under the passenger seat, or wherever those ivory tower engineers have decided to place it in your particular car). Sulfuric acid batteries are divided into two types—those that can have water added to them, and those that are sealed and can not have water added. You need to discover which type your car has in it—because a water adding battery needs a small bit of maintenance, while a sealed battery does not. IF YOUR CAR HAS A BATTERY THAT NEEDS WATER ADDED, BE SURE TO CHECK THE FLUID LEVEL IN THE BATTERY OCCASIONALLY. For most normal operating conditions, checking it once every couple of months is sufficient. It's very simple, if you care to do it yourself. Just remove the six battery caps from the top of the battery and look inside. If the battery acid inside is sufficient, you will see nothing but liquid floating inside the battery cells. If the acid is low, you will see many small lead plates arranged in rows. When you see these rows, pour DISTILLED WATER into each cell until it reaches the full mark. The full mark is just below the top of the battery cell— when you reach it, the liquid level will slightly bulge as it hits the ridge. If you don't want to bother with the checking yourself, simply remind your mechanic to check it whenever any other maintenance, such as an oil change, is being done. Sulfuric acid is H_2SO_4 (two atoms of hydrogen, one atom of sulfur, and four atoms of oxygen), and while operating a car, some of these atoms become gaseous and evaporate out of the battery over time. This is why you need to check the battery level occasionally. Since water is H_2O (two atoms of hydrogen and one atom of water), it can be placed back in the battery to replenish the atoms that have been lost by evaporation. The reason I advise you to use distilled water is because it contains nothing but hydrogen and oxygen—normal tap water contains many minerals that could begin to destroy your battery when they react with the sulfuric acid inside. You don't have to worry about causing an explosion if you use normal tap water, it will just shorten your battery's lifespan. If you're stuck in the middle of nowhere and discover your battery is very low on fluid, you're better off adding tap water than by leaving the battery low. An almost dry battery will burn out faster than one that has tap water added to it.

Here you may very well ask, why don't all cars have batteries that are sealed and don't need to be checked? A few years back, most cars did come with sealed batteries. But these batteries still contain sulfuric acid—they are merely redesigned and have smaller vent holes for the gases to escape from. The battery acid does evaporate from these batteries—it just takes longer for the batteries to go dry. And when they do go dry, you can't add water to them—you have to go and purchase a new battery. To compensate for this evaporation, some battery companies even tried an acid gel battery. But these batteries had so many design flaws that they were soon pulled off the market. If you are very poor about having your battery level checked, you are probably better off buying a sealed battery. With no maintenance, a sealed battery will certainly outlast an unsealed battery. But if you have the battery level checked occasionally, an unsealed battery should give you a longer lifespan. And if you check the battery inventory at most battery and auto parts stores, you will soon discover that the unsealed batteries are more numerous and cheaper. Many stores no longer even carry sealed batteries.

Your car's alternator and the electrical system.

The alternator in your car generates electricity that is used to both recharge the battery and to run the car's various electrical systems. In most modern cars the alternator and the regulator (the device that regulates the amount of electricity generated) are contained in the same unit. This unit is just commonly known as the alternator, and it's a sealed unit. The only real maintenance you need to perform is the following: Please keep your car from going on a swim. Immersing the car's alternator under water will greatly shorten its lifespan (and its circuitry).

Your alternator is driven by a fan belt. The fan belt should be inspected for cracks, and be periodically adjusted to ensure proper operation. With correct fan belt tension becoming more and more

122

complex, most people are better off leaving this to a mechanic—because if you overtighten fan belts, you can damage very expensive parts. It isn't something that needs to be done very often. Modern fan belts are very well made and will often last over sixty thousand miles. Just have them checked by your mechanic when he's doing other maintenance, or right before you begin that summer vacation drive.

Your car's computer systems.

The electrical systems of modern cars are controlled by sophisticated computer driven systems. Considering the immense heat and humidity that they are subjected to, it's truly amazing that they work as well as they do. Just imagine how your pampered home or office computer would hold up if it was taken out of its temperature and humidity controlled home or office and was stuck inside the heat and humidity of a car! In the summertime sun, the temperature in a car can easily top 130 degrees, and the humidity after a rainstorm can be well over 90 percent. In the winter, the temperature can go well below freezing, and ice can form on the circuitry. You'd probably be lucky to get your home computer to even boot up under such conditions. But your car's various computer systems keep humming along—even those sensors on the engine that can exceed 450 degrees!

There are only two things that you need to do to ensure these systems continue on their merry way:

1.Never subject them to water in any shape or form. Many computer systems are placed under the seats of your car. I've seen jumbo drinks of soda which had been inadvertently spilled under a car seat—they destroyed computer control units that cost eight hundred dollars. I've seen cars that were driven through floodwater that "only got the floor mats a little wet." This too had done extensive computer damage. Be sure to keep your car's interior away from the beach—no matter how hot it is.

2. If your car battery goes dead and you need to have your car jumped-started, be sure it is done correctly. If the battery poles are reversed, the computer systems of your car will be decimated. Make sure that the positive terminal of the one car is connected to the positive terminal of the other car—and that the negative terminal is connected only to the other negative terminal. It's a very simple process, but I've seen it botched up many times by unknowing motorists or foolish "mechanics". The last warning is one that you must tell any professional attempting

to jump start your car. Some assistance vehicles have electrical boosters that can "hot shot" your car with 24 volts (instead of the normal 12). Never allow anyone to hot shot a car—it would cause computer damage beyond your wildest dreams. If your car will not start with a normal jump, either purchase a new battery, or have it towed to a mechanic. Unless you happen to be a millionaire who doesn't care about money (a contradiction in itself), don't ever allow anyone to hot shot your car.

H. Your Car's Clutch.

If your car has a standard transmission, a clutch is used to connect the engine to the transmission. The clutch itself consists of three main parts—the clutch plate, the clutch disc, and the clutch throw-out bearing. The part that generally wears out first is the clutch disc. The disc is covered with a lining that is usually the same material that is used in your car's brake linings. In the course of everyday driving, this lining eventually wears out. When the lining begins to reach the end of its lifespan, the clutch starts to slip. Then it's time to have the clutch replaced in your car.

You may ask, what does a slipping clutch feel like, and how can I prevent the clutch from wearing out too soon? Well, a slipping clutch feels exactly as its name implies—the power from the car's engine does not reach the wheels because the clutch disc is slipping inside the clutch pressure plate. When you accelerate hard in a car that has a slipping clutch, the engine will rev up quickly—but the speedometer will not increase its speed as fast as it normally does. The slipping clutch does transmit some power to the wheels (especially when it has just begun to slip), but it also loses some of the engine's power. When the clutch is just beginning to slip, this loss of power is most noticed as the car is accelerated hard at highway speeds (55 mph and up). And it will be even more noticeable when accelerating up hill at highway speeds. It is better to have a clutch replaced soon after a reasonable amount of slippage is noticed—because this will prevent worn-out clutch parts from wearing down to bare metal and causing more expensive damage. I've had customers who waited until their clutch was so worn-out that their car had to be towed over to me for repairs. Instead of a three hundred dollar bill, their bills have often topped six hundred. And the extra time they were able to safely drive their cars only amounted to a few thousand miles at best.

So how can you prevent the premature wearing-out of your car's clutch? If you have a line operated clutch, you or your mechanic should check its adjustment once or twice a year. It's a very simple process and only takes a couple minutes. A correctly adjusted clutch will add thousands of miles to its lifespan. If a clutch is adjusted too tightly, it acts as if you are driving the car with your foot always planted on the clutch pedal. As most car clutches tighten themselves up as they wear, you will have to have a line operated clutch checked and loosened up (if needed) every few months or so. But fortunately for you, most cars today have hydraulically operated clutches, which are self-adjusting. They adjust themselves with hydraulic fluid as you drive. The only thing you need to do is check the little clutch fluid reservoir once in a while to ensure that the system has plenty of fluid. You can do this whenever you have the brake fluid level checked (they both use the exact same fluid).

For most of you out there with standard transmission cars, the best way to get the longest lifespan out of your clutch has more to do with personal driving habits. To get the longest life out of your clutch, try to use these tips as often as possible:

1. Do not make a practice of downshifting your car—it will only wear out your clutch, your engine, and your transmission faster. Every time you downshift hard from a higher gear to a lower gear, the clutch gets a hard jolt while the engine and transmission have to spin much faster than is normally needed. Of course, if you find yourself in an emergency situation where you must slow down quickly, by all means downshift the car and firmly apply the brakes. But don't make downshifting something that you do "all the time", because it will make the clutch, the engine, and the transmission wear out prematurely. Some of you may want to drive like you're vying for the lead in the Indianapolis 500—but remember this: Race cars have their clutches replaced after every race, along with complete tear-downs of their engines and transmissions. Unless your personal driving is sponsored by a major company, I would advise you to keep downshifting out of your portfolio.

2. Whenever your car is going to be sitting for more than thirty seconds or so, you should put your car in neutral and take your foot off the clutch. This cuts down on wear and tear to the clutch throw-out bearing, the clutch pressure plate, and the clutch hydraulic system. It's a simple habit to get into—unless you happen to reside in San Francisco and have to use your clutch as a permanent hill-climber.

3. Operate your clutch smoothly—pick your foot up from the clutch pedal in one firm but smooth action. The smoother you engage your

car's clutch, the longer it will last. I've personally seen smooth shifters get 150,000 miles out of a clutch (though admittedly they did an awful lot of strictly highway driving—where no shifting is involved at all). Don't smash your foot down on the clutch pedal to shift gears, and then jerk it back off to engage the clutch. You may like the sound of squealing tires as you shift gears, but your car certainly doesn't appreciate it and will eventually tell you so with an early repair bill (if the police don't get you first).

I. Your Car's Air Conditioning System.

If you live in a hot or extremely humid area, your car's air conditioning system is probably very important to you (unless you happen to be on a sweat-it-out diet). More and more cars are being equipped with air conditioning—I know of people even in Buffalo who just can't live without its cooling breeze in the summer. And here in hot, humid Texas, I've had customers sell their old cars when the AC systems broke down permanently (with the repair cost being more than the older car's entire value). So what can you do to ensure your car's AC system does not die a premature death?

To begin with, car AC systems are not like house AC systems—they do not have filters on the air intake duct that you should change once a month. Car systems have a much higher level of air flow than house systems, and their AC evaporator coils are basically self-cleaning. The combination of high air flow and condensed water serves to clean dust off the car AC evaporator and keeps it blowing cool air day after day. This is a good thing, because accessing the evaporator coils inside the dash of most cars is a very time consuming (and expensive) job. Many of you who have parked your air conditioned cars under pine trees for long periods of time have probably discovered this. The pine needles will often get sucked into the air conditioning air intake ducts, and these needles will often stick inside the evaporator case. When enough of these needles are collected, they create a little dam that plugs up the evaporator drain plug. Then the water created by condensation begins to drip inside the car. To repair this leaking, the AC evaporator case has to be dismantled and physically cleaned out—a very expensive procedure. Most cars have air intake screens to keep foreign objects out of the AC evaporator,but pine needles are often thin enough to sneak by them. So rule number one for AC maintenance is to keep your car parked away from pine trees (or other small falling objects).

There is no real physical maintenance that you can perform on your AC system other than inspecting the fan belt that drives the AC compressor. Have it checked occasionally, just like you do the alternator fan belt. If it is out of adjustment and squeals occasionally, have its tension readjusted. The rest of your car's AC system is a sealed unit that should not be tinkered with by anyone except a good mechanic. Not only could an untrained person really botch things up—it's now against the law for them to work on car AC systems (due to environmental laws attempting to protect the ozone layer).

But there are a few bits of information I can give you here to keep your AC system from causing you unnecessarily high repair bills. If your AC is blowing cold air all the time, and doesn't make any odd noises when operating, just leave it alone and be content. But if it begins to operate poorly, have your trusted mechanic take a look at it. If it blows cold in the early hours of the day, but gets less cold as the day heats up, it may be low on freon. If it drips water inside the car, the evaporator needs cleaning out. And if it begins to make strange noises under the hood, it may need compressor work. Let your mechanic look at it and tell you what is needed—especially if you hear strange noises coming from the system. Because some noises are telling you to fix the problem now before more major damage is done—and some noises just tell you the system is getting old, but is still performing ok. As an example, some Volvos in the mid eighties used a Japanese AC compressor that had a nasty habit of groaning when just a few years old. When the AC switch is turned on, these cars emit a low-pitched groan that increases as the engine increases its speed. When the AC switch is turned off, the groaning stops. I have seen this groaning go on in these cars for years, yet the AC systems continued to function properly. In these particular cars, the groaning is just something that the drivers should learn to live with (unless they wish to spend 750 dollars for peace and quiet). If you have any qualms about you car's AC system, take it to your trusted mechanic and learn what is cool and what isn't.

J. Your Car's Fan Belts.

The fan belts under the hood of your car serve to drive various accessories—power steering pumps, air conditioning compressors, water pumps, anti-pollution smog pumps, and so on. They are made of rubber composites—so they need occasional adjustments and eventual replacement when they're worn out. Today's fan belts are better made than their predecessors. They will often last 50,000 miles or longer—especially if your car has a Unibelt system (where your car has only one extremely long belt that drives everything). If your particular car does have a Unibelt system, it probably is even self-adjusting and does not require periodic tinkering. The only thing I advise those of you with Unibelt systems to do is to go out and purchase a spare belt at your local auto parts store. Throw it in your trunk for an emergency spare—it should only cost you twenty dollars or so. This Unibelt drives every single accessory on your car's engine, so if it breaks, you'll lose power steering, your water pump (the car will begin to overheat), and your alternator (the car will begin to lose electrical power). Having a correct spare in your trunk will make replacement much easier—even if you don't want to attempt it yourself. (For those of you brave enough to attempt replacement yourself, most cars have a Unibelt routing diagram stuck under the hood somewhere).

In cars that have independent fan belt systems with two or more belts, just have them inspected occasionally for cracks and signs of looseness. Fan belts today are generally designed with cooling fins on them, so they can last a long time (50,000 miles is common in many cars today). When the car's oil is being changed, just have them inspected and readjusted if needed. And if your present belts have more than 50,000 miles on them, you might just go and have them changed out before taking that big trip to the Grand Canyon. It isn't very expensive, and can give you peace of mind for the next 50,000 miles.

K. Your Car's Paint, Bodywork, And Interior

You all want your car to look its best for as long as possible, but no one wants to spend their life chained to a car door with a bucket and a can of car wax. The good news is that you don't have to be a slave to your car, or spend tons of money enslaving others to do the task. Your car really only needs to be waxed once a year—preferably in the early spring before things begin getting hot. The wax serves to seal in the elasticity of the car's paint—to prevent the paint from fading and cracking. Once a year, you should have your car hand washed and dried. Then the car should be waxed thoroughly and buffed out. If you really want to be a perfectionist, you can rewax the car on the next day. That is It. And according to a good bodyman friend of mine, it really doesn't matter what type of wax you are using. He said to ignore all the various products out there in auto accessory land which claim to last for years (or even for the car's lifetime). Just use any auto part store wax that you feel comfortable with, and wax your car once a year. Of course if your car becomes subjected to rather nasty forces of nature (such as an aerial bombardment by a flock of seagulls), you may have to rewax the sections that sustained the heaviest damage.

The best maintenance you can do for your car's appearance is to keep it out of the sun. Everyone knows that a garaged car has a much higher

128

resale value than one left out in the elements. The sun with its ultraviolet rays will fade paint over time, and do even nastier things to the interior of your car. Many people now use those sun shades that fold out to cover the car's windshield and dash. They are certainly better than nothing, but parking the car in a covered shady spot is much better. The heat build-up inside a sun drenched car is immense—even with a sun shade covering the dash. But if you are unable to park your car in a nice shady spot, at least you can prevent much of the damage that sunlight causes. Simply purchase a spray bottle of liquid wax and apply it liberally to any vinyl or plastic surface your car has. (As with most things in the car world, there are scores of liquid spray waxes out there. Just pick a brand you like and stick with it). Do this every other time you have the car washed if you want to be cautious. You can spray the dash, the door panels, the rubberized bumpers, and any vinyl trim your car may have. And as a special note for those out there with leather seats, I would advise you to go out and purchase a special leather treatment salve to keep those expensive derriere cushions well tanned. The extra cost is nothing compared to reupholstering them.

As for your car's bodywork, the best maintenance you can do for those fenders and bumpers is to avoid running into large objects. But when your car does meet up with smaller flying objects (such as rocks and errant hubcaps), have the small dents and dings touched up before they become large cancerous rust holes. If you don't want to go to the expense of a body shop, at least sand off the damaged area and paint it with primer. Maybe even attempt to paint small areas over with one of those touch-up paint tubes you can get at the auto parts store (yes, I know they never match perfectly, but they are very cheap and will help stop rust from forming).

And lastly, if you car gets a coating of road tar or other nasty substance, please don't try to clean it off with a can of carburetor cleaning spray. Aside from stripping off your nice wax job, it will start to rub the paint off along with the tar. Go out and purchase a can of tar/bug remover at any auto parts store. It's only a couple dollars, and it was made specifically for such a job. You might even think about stashing a can in your trunk for future "emergencies" if you're extremely fastidious.

L. Your Car's Air Filter.

All cars have air filters that keep airborne contaminants from getting inside the engine and causing damage. In the olden days these filters were simple oil baths, where the oil had to be checked very rigorously and changed out every few thousand miles. Today's air filters are practically maintenance-free when compared to these dinosaurs. Their paper filters have a large surface area which gives them a long lifespan—some will last 50,000 miles or more. Car manufacturers give different mileage figures for the suggested mileage to change out your car's air filter—but the true time to change your filter depends more upon driving environment than actual mileage. If you drive in areas that have a large concentration of airborne contaminants, the filter will get dirty faster and will need changing earlier. And if you drive in rather dust-free areas, they may last even longer.

So how can you tell when it's the right time to replace the filter? The simplest way is to have your filter physically inspected twice a year or so. It should be a simple task, unless your car happened to be designed by by one of those nasty engineers who decided to hide the filter canister in a totally inaccessible area underneath half of the car. (There are a few turbo charged cars out there with filters that take even a mechanic over an hour to access.) Hopefully your car is not one of these monsters—because it only takes a minute in most cars to remove the air filter from its container. Once the air filter is removed, see if it's covered with filth and slime. If it is, simply throw it away and buy another. But if it isn't obviously covered with crud, whack it against the nearest solid object (tree, car bumper, etc.) to remove any dust or dead dragonflies that may be stuck in it. Act like an old timer beating a rug with a stick to remove all the dirt. When you've finished, simply look through the filter at the sun. If you can see the light through the filter, then it's ok to use it over. (If the sun isn't out, you can use a 100 watt lightbulb as a substitute.) If the light is blocked out by the filter, then go ahead and buy another one.

And as a special note, a few late model cars have returned to a reusable air filter design, in an effort to reduce the garbage waste created by throwing away old paper filters. These filters have special directions for proper maintenance printed on their canisters under the car's hood. Simply follow these directions when oiling or cleaning these reusable filters.

M. Stay Away From All Possible Hare-Brained Auto Maintenance Schemes.

As a final note, I'll leave you with a warning—PLEASE, UNDER NO CIRCUMSTANCES, LISTEN TO ANYONE'S HARE-BRAINED SCHEME ON HOW YOU CAN SAVE MONEY MAINTAINING YOUR CAR. Over the years, I've heard some real doozers involving how to save money by maintaining your car in a cheaper fashion. Everything from add-on water injection systems that supposedly increased gas mileage, to oil additive treatments that would "rebuild your engine as you drive". Some of these schemes are harmless in themselves (though you'd be wasting money on them), but some can be dangerous to the health of your car.

As perhaps the most bizarre example anyone could imagine, one of my customers had just returned from a trip out West. While travelling in Oregon, he met a gas station attendant who gave him the following hare-brained advice. He claimed that adding three mothballs to every ten gallons of regular unleaded gas would turn it into high-test unleaded gas. The attendant said to use only 100 percent Naphthalene mothballs, because this would boost the gasoline octane up to 95 (the level of high-test gasoline). My customer hadn't tried it yet, because he wanted my advice. Not being a chemist myself, I called up one of my regular customers, who just happened to be a chemical engineer at an oil refinery. I was told that the mothballs probably would have other ingredients in them that could possibly clog up the fuel system—but that this was just a minor problem. The MAJOR problem far outweighed this small side effect—because mixing mothballs with gasoline would create Napalm (that nasty fireball substance made famous by the Vietnam War). Not too many people would feel safe driving around with an auto-igniting substance floating around in their gas tank.

Admittedly most hare-brained schemes won't result in you "going up in flames", but they may help bring your car to a screeching halt or an early grave. My advice is to ignore any hare-brained schemes that you hear about—or even better, to write them down and discuss them with your trusted mechanic. We all need a good laugh in these trying times.

We at On The Road Press are dedicated to publishing informational books that are of great current interest to the general public. We know there are many of you out there just overflowing with information that people would give their eye teeth for (making a 12.95 paperback price seem inconsequential). If you are presently writing such a book, or are planning on doing so, please drop us a line at On The Road Press, P.O. Box 540326, Houston, Texas, 77254-0326. We will gladly accept manuscripts on a wide range of informational topics—everything from advice books to zestful living books.

We would like to hear from you. If you have some interesting car tips, outrageous car stories, any car questions , or great car advice to share, please mail us a letter or post card.

We at On the Road Press are going to produce a newsletter called "The Mechanic's Voice". It will have letters and car questions answered by Scott, plus some stories on up to date maintenance problems and possible rip-offs to avoid.

If you are interested in receiving "The Mechanic's Voice" quarterly newsletter, please send a check or money order for $11.95 to: On The Road Press, P.O. Box 540326, Houston, Texas, 77254-0326.

Special Charter Subscriber Offer:
You can now get your first year of "The Mechanic's Voice" newsletter for the special charter subscription price of only $9.95 for the first year (4 issues). So take advantage of this special offer today and enjoy the tips, funny stories and great advice all year.

Name _____

Address _____

_____

_____

_____